Wisdom *of*
The Carpenter:

365

Prayers and
Meditations of Jesus

Ron Miller

Introduction by Marcus Borg

In memory of my father
Harry O. Miller
November 7, 1906–April 8, 2002
with love and gratitude

Introduction

by Marcus Borg

I am pleased to write an introduction to this collection of Jesus' wisdom teachings. There are several reasons. Ron Miller's work is informed by contemporary scholarship on Jesus and the gospels, even as it serves a meditative and devotional purpose: a short saying of Jesus for each day of the year, followed by a brief comment and a short prayer.

I like the format. Seeing the short sayings of Jesus with a lot of white space around them encourages a certain way of reading them. I am reminded of the first time, now over twenty-five years ago, that I read the wisdom sayings of Lao Tzu, a sixth-century BCE Chinese wisdom teacher. His teachings are collected in the *Tao Te Ching* (pronounced "dow de ching"), a small volume sometimes called in English "The Way of Lao Tzu." Like Jesus, Lao Tzu taught "a way," "a path," a way of living that is deeper than behavior.

Lao Tzu's sayings are compact, sometimes just a line or two, sometimes several lines, but never long enough to cover a whole page. I read Lao Tzu by the light of an oil lamp, and I still vividly remember the effect of seeing his brief enigmatic teachings surrounded by so much white space. The space invited pausing, lingering, reflecting, puzzling, chewing, munching, often spending several minutes on a single page. Sometimes I even felt that I was "getting it," flickers of enlightenment glimmering in the lamp light.

We seldom see the sayings of Jesus presented in this manner, and my hope is that the effect on readers may be similar to what I experienced with Lao Tzu. Of course, Lao Tzu's teachings had the advantage of being unfamiliar. For many people in Western culture, the sayings of Jesus suffer from familiarity and domestication: we've heard them before, and we most likely have heard particular (and often quite conventional) meanings imparted to them. Miller's book helps to counter familiarity and domestication. Not only does the format invite a different kind of reflection, his translations are often fresh and arresting.

There is another reason I like the format. Providing a saying for each day of the year encourages daily devotional practice. For people who take the life of the spirit and the life of the heart seriously, there is real value in daily practice. I know its value in my own life: when I begin a day with a period of devotional reading and meditation, my day goes better. Indeed, value may be too weak a word. For many of us, such practice addresses a need and feeds a hunger. We do not live by bread alone, even though the wisdom of the carpenter also tells us that bread matters greatly.

Jesus' wisdom teaching takes two classic forms: parables and aphorisms. Jesus' parables were provocative and often surprising short stories that invited reflection, and his aphorisms were brief, memorable, arresting sayings. They are invitational forms of speech, inviting people to see in a particular way, or to see something they might not otherwise see.

Thus, one of the most certain things that we know about Jesus is that he was a story-teller and a speaker of great "one-liners." Moreover, he used these invitational forms of speech

to suggest a way of seeing that was most often quite different from conventional wisdom. Conventional wisdom is "what
everybody knows," the cultural consensus of a given time and
place. Jesus' stories and one-liners undermine the conventional
wisdom of his time and every time, and invite us, like his original hearers, to see life quite differently. In this sense, they are
subversive wisdom.

This book concentrates on Jesus' one-liners, and its pre-
sentation of Jesus' teaching as short sayings isolated from each
other corresponds to the way Jesus himself often taught. To
explain: In the gospels, the short sayings of Jesus are most often
collected into a series of sayings. This is perfectly natural in
written documents.

But this is not how Jesus would have spoken them. Jesus
was an oral teacher. As an oral teacher, Jesus would not have
strung a bunch of unrelated sayings together in an extended series. To follow a great one-liner like "Leave the dead to bury the
dead" with another one-liner like "No one who puts his hand
to the plow and looks back is fit for the Kingdom of God" with
another one-liner like "Foxes have holes, and birds have nests,
but humans have nowhere to lay their heads" would have been
pedagogically counterproductive. It is impossible to imagine in
an oral situation. His hearers needed time to digest what had
just been said. The format of this book makes it possible for us
to have that time.

Like other scholars, Miller is aware of the distinction between the historical Jesus and the Jesus we meet on the pages of
the gospel. The former (sometimes called "the pre-Easter Jesus)
is the subject of the quest for the historical Jesus. The Jesus we
meet on the pages of the gospels (called variously "the post-
Easter Jesus" or "the canonical Jesus") is what Jesus became in

the experience and developing traditions of the early Christian movement in the decades after Jesus' death.

Miller (quite properly) does not confine himself to the historical Jesus. Thus, in some of these sayings, we hear the voice of Jesus, or at least an echo of it. In others, we hear what he had become in the experience and thought of his first followers.

Jesus was more than a wisdom teacher, of course. In the judgment of most historical scholars, he was also a remarkable healer—more healing stories are told about him than about any other figure in the Jewish tradition.

Most scholars also see him as a prophet, like the great social prophets of the Hebrew Bible, figures like Amos, Micah, and Jeremiah. Like them, Jesus was a voice of God-intoxicated religious social protest against "the powers that be"—an economically exploitative domination system not only ruled but designed by elites of wealth and power in their own narrow self-interest.

And, in the judgment of some scholars (including me), Jesus was also a Jewish mystic for whom God was an experiential reality. Indeed, I think Jesus' mystical experience, coupled with a brilliant and poetic intellect, is the best explanation of his wisdom teaching. He taught differently because he had seen differently.

For Christians, both in the first century and today, Jesus is more than even this, of course. In the language of Christian affirmation, he is also the messiah, Lord, Son of God, Word of God, lamb of God, light of the world, bread of life, way and truth, resurrection and life, and more. The carpenter from Nazareth made it big.

And, of course, he was killed. Even though Jesus' death is at the very center of Christian perceptions of Jesus, we seldom take sufficiently seriously that he didn't simply die—he was executed. Christians live in the only major religious tradition in the world whose founder was executed by established authority. We have domesticated that fact in many ways—by speaking of it as the will of God, as the necessary sacrifice for sin, and so forth.

But it was not Jesus' wisdom teaching alone that got him killed. Indeed, had he been only a wisdom teacher, he almost certainly would not have been arrested and executed. We need to remember that there was something about this figure that moved the authorities—the elites of power and wealth—to do away with him. They were not simply mistaken in their perception of him as an advocate of a vision that threatened the "normalcy" of the social order they had created. "The wisdom of the carpenter" is the wisdom of one who was executed by the powers that rule this world. Jesus' wisdom does subvert the normalcy of life.

In his novel *The Last Temptation of Christ*, Nikos Kazantzakis imagines that Jesus as a carpenter sometimes made crosses for the Romans to use to execute Jews suspected of subversion. It is a haunting image: Jesus making his own cross.

Of course, it is fiction, but metaphorically it works well. The wisdom of the carpenter is crystallized in "the way of the cross": "If any want to become my followers, let them deny themselves and take up their cross and follow me" (Mark 8:34). And the wisdom of Jesus, along with what else he was, led to the cross. The story of Jesus, and the wisdom of Jesus, is both personal and political, both spiritual and social.

I welcome you to this book. It is the wisdom of a Jewish carpenter from Nazareth who is also, for Christians, the light of the world and the bread of life. May it enlighten and nourish your days.

Preface

Yehoshua Ben Yosef was called Yeshu. Since the gospels were written in Greek, and since there is no "sh" sound in that language, he became known to the Gentile world as Jesus. His brief teaching career took place some two thousand years ago in Israel. One gospel identifies him as a carpenter by trade. In the world of that time, the term could include any kind of day laborer, working either with stone or wood. As far as we know, he never wrote anything nor did he travel more than one hundred miles from where he was born.

Why then does this carpenter continue to exert a profound influence on countless human beings in every part of the globe? How is his message to be understood in the new era we are entering? Does his wisdom have relevance to a world whose calendar has passed the 2000th anniversary of his birth? These are the questions underlying this endeavor. This calendar book is an attempt to present Jesus and his teachings in a way that is meaningful for the new millennium we have entered.

For some thirty years now, I have been teaching in the college classroom, in churches and synagogues, and in adult education centers. I have noticed that even among Christians who are regular church goers, the teachings of Jesus often remain unknown. Relating to Jesus as the one who redeems them by his death and resurrection, some Christians neglect Jesus as the one who teaches them in parables and aphorisms. Seeing the purpose of Christianity as providing a ticket to heaven and the happiness of the next world, some Christians overlook the wisdom of Jesus' teachings for living in this world.

The book's format provides for a daily reflection consisting of three parts: a saying attributed to Jesus; a brief commentary; and a prayer for the day. In some instances the saying chosen for a particular day corresponds to the date (e.g., Christmas) or the time of year (e.g., the year's beginning or end). No calendar year, however, is included so that the book can be used for any year and for many years in a row.

These teachings of Jesus are not the exclusive property of Christians. They belong to the world and have often been better understood and practiced by Hindus like Mahatma Gandhi, Buddhists like the Dalai Lama, and Jews like Martin Buber than by millions of us who call ourselves Christians. Whatever one's religious background, pondering even one of these teachings can lead to a profound life transformation. The brilliant Francis Xavier's life was turned around when Ignatius of Loyola quoted to him the saying of Jesus: "What does it profit you to gain the whole world but lose your soul?"

Marcus Borg makes the point in his *Meeting Jesus Again for the First Time* that Jesus was a teacher of subversive wisdom. There's a significant difference between conventional wisdom and subversive wisdom. Conventional wisdom is the wisdom we hardly need to talk about since we all take it for granted, such as the underlying assumption of our society that happiness is measured by the amount of one's material possessions. Conventional wisdom is thus the voice of the status quo, a "wisdom" that often supports the most destructive elements of a society: its elitism, racism, and sexism. Subversive wisdom, on the other hand, deliberately challenges conventional wisdom. Consequently, teachers of subversive wisdom—like Socrates, Gandhi, Martin Luther King, Jr., and Jesus himself—are often killed by the defenders of conventional wisdom.

Jesus taught in Aramaic and his words were passed on in the Greek language of the Christian Testament. The sayings of Jesus quoted in this volume are taken not only from the four canonical gospels (Matthew, Mark, Luke, and John) but from other gospels from the early years of Christian history, especially The Gospel of Thomas. When citing Thomas, I will use the translation from the edition of Thomas cited in Further Reading on page 385. Otherwise, the translations found here are my own and I offer them with the realization that "every translator is a traitor." I take liberties with the text that go beyond their literal meanings but attempt to point to their essence.

There is another gospel hidden in the texts of Matthew and Luke. It consists of passages found in these two gospels but not found in Mark. Some German scholars concluded more than a hundred years ago that Matthew and Luke, in addition to having Mark at their disposal, had another written source. Seeking a name for this source, they used the letter "Q" to identify this hypothesized document, since the German word for "source" is *Quelle*. When I quote from Q, I will identify the saying by the number found in the edition cited in Further Reading on page 385.

I do not believe that all the words quoted here were spoken by the historical Jesus. Too many translations and editings separate us from this Jewish teacher for us to have the certitude of exact quotation. I have tried, however, to include teachings attributed to Jesus that, at least in my judgment, are in the spirit of his message. Like every scholar of this literature, I have developed a sense of what I consider Jesus' authentic voice.

The idea for this book came from a former student, Darryl Rose. He noticed that the teachings of Jesus were conspicuously absent from the plethora of little instruction books found in bookstores. This writing is an attempt to redress that imbalance, and I am grateful to Darryl for the impetus to tackle this project. This manuscript was first published in a limited edition of one thousand copies by Common Ground, an adult education center for religious study and dialogue in the Greater Chicago area. After the Common Ground edition sold out, Ulysses Press agreed to republish the manuscript and I am grateful to Ray Riegert of Ulysses Press for his help in bringing this book to a larger audience. It was Marcus Borg who first put me in touch with Ray Riegert and I appreciate that contact, as well as Marcus' willingness to write an Introduction for this volume.

I want to thank the many people who have collaborated on this volume: Jim Kenney, Executive Director of Common Ground; Mason Wiley, former Board Member of Common Ground; Lisa Wagner, Jason Neal, and Michael Froelich, graduates of Lake Forest College. Paul Tzirides, a current student at Lake Forest College, worked with me in revising the manuscript for Ulysses Press. Noel Black and John Crosby, both poets and dear friends, merit special thanks for reading the final manuscript and making helpful comments both on the language and on the theology. Finally, I want to thank Matt Patterson, another alumnus of Lake Forest College and Board Member of Common Ground, whose summer research project for two years was to work with me in the preparation of this book. Matt and I have been colleagues in this project and much of what is written here reflects his insight and vision.

Ronald H. Miller
Chair of the Religion Department,
Lake Forest College
Co-Director, Common Ground

September 1, 2002

January 1

Love and goodness are the beginning of the way.
Dialogue of the Savior 28:1-2

Beginnings are important, the first days of a new year, the first steps of a journey. They can also be challenging. A German proverb reminds us, "Alle Anfang ist schwer" (Every beginning is difficult). But if we begin with love and goodness, with God, the way will be clear.

Daily Prayer

Thank you for allowing me to begin this year in You, the source and fountain of all love and goodness.

January 2

Peace be with you.
Luke 24:36

The Risen Jesus appears again and again to various disciples with these comforting words of peace. The night is over and a new day has dawned. He is truly risen and sits now at the right hand of his Heavenly Parent.

Daily Prayer

Let me know your peace today and your life-giving presence.

January 3

Do not fear; only believe.
Mark 5:36

The opposite of fear is a profound faith enabling us to let go of our insecurities so that we can trust the larger mystery of the divine. Only this deep trust can displace the gnawing fear that so often holds us prisoner.

Daily Prayer

May my trust in You today overcome every fear on my path.

January 4

I am sending upon you what my Heavenly Parent promised;
so stay here in the city until you have been clothed with
power from on high.
Luke 24:49

Although Jesus must be removed from their earthly realm
of experience, the newly formed Jesus community will be
strengthened by receiving the promised Holy Spirit. They
will indeed be "clothed with power from on high." So will all
human beings who strive to walk in the path of truth.

Daily Prayer

*Clothe me today with Your spirit and with power from on
high.*

January 5

You did not choose me but I chose you.
John 15:16a

All the great spiritual wisdoms assure us that the initiative comes from the divine. Ours is always a way rooted in response. The Christian community consists of those people called by God to walk a spiritual path centered on Jesus and his teachings. But all of humankind can benefit from this teacher of truth.

Daily Prayer

Thank You for choosing me to walk on the path where You have placed my feet.

January 6

I am the vine; you are the branches. Those who abide in me
and I in them bear much fruit.
John 15:5

Like St. Paul's image of many members forming one body,
Jesus here uses the organic image of a vine and its branches.
These are powerful metaphors for the close union between
Jesus and the community bearing his name. Certainly all peo-
ple of good will are vital branches of this heavenly vine.

Daily Prayer

*Help me to abide in You this day so that I may bear fruit
that lasts.*

January 7

No difference is to be made between the greatest and
the youngest of all, between those who command and
those who serve.
Luke 22:26

Elitism has no place at God's table. We are all brothers and
sisters with only God as our Heavenly Parent. The community that Jesus calls into being should not exercise power over
others; its goal is rather that others be empowered. And this
should be the goal of every community moving our planet to
greater spiritual life.

Daily Prayer

*Help me today to avoid patronizing people or dealing with
them from any sense of my own superiority.*

January 8

The first commandment is to love the Lord your God with all
your heart, soul, mind, and strength.
Mark 12:30

Jesus quotes the Torah (Deuteronomy 6), citing the "Ve-hafta"
prayer of his own Jewish liturgy as articulating God's central commandment. With God as the cornerstone of our life,
everything else will find its rightful place.

Daily Prayer

I love You. Let that be enough.

January 9

The second commandment is to love your neighbor
as yourself.
Mark 12:31

Jesus again quotes the Torah (Leviticus 19): its explicit commandment to love our neighbor and its implicit commandment to love ourselves. The neighbor, whoever is next to us in
any given moment, merits our unconditional good will.

Daily Prayer

*Help me to show unconditional good will to all people today.
As Your children, we are all brothers and sisters.*

January 10

This is my body which is given for you. Do this for a
commemoration of me.
Luke 22:19

Sharing the matzah (flat bread prepared without yeast)
with his friends, Jesus identifies himself with this bread that
is broken. He wants the community that will one day bear his
name to remember him in this ritual act of breaking bread.

Daily Prayer

*Help me to realize that as I serve the world, I too am called
to be a bread that is broken to nurture others today.*

January 11

This cup that is poured out for you is the new covenant
in my blood.
Luke 22:20

First, bread is broken. Now, wine is poured out. Images of
suffering and death; and yet, in both instances a community
is thereby being nurtured and served. This is the mystery of
the Eucharist ("the thanksgiving"), the Lord's Supper, the
communion: only broken bread can be eaten; only poured out
wine can be drunk.

Daily Prayer

*Help me to be ready to be broken and poured out today
for others.*

January 12

Love your enemies. Do good to those who hate you. Bless
those who curse you. Pray for those who treat you badly.
Gospel Q 14

Loving our enemies really means losing them as enemies and
finding them as fellow human beings, our hidden brothers and
sisters. Praying for our "enemies" means affirming their basic
humanity and wanting their growth and happiness.

Daily Prayer

Take me through this day finding no enemies.

January 13

Let your word be a simple yes or no; anything more than
that comes from the evil one.
Matthew 5:37

Backing our words up with oaths and elaborate assurances
only lessens our credibility. So too does all the equivocating
that fills our conversations. It's refreshing to meet someone
whose speech is straightforward and honest.

Daily Prayer

*Help me to be candid today, speaking the truth in love
on every occasion.*

January 14

Ask and it will be given to you; seek and you will find; knock
and the door will be opened for you.
Gospel Q 35

No prayer is unanswered if we are truly seeking God's will.
God is always there for us and the answer to our prayer is
always the fullest presence of God that we are able to
receive in that moment.

Daily Prayer

*Let me ask eagerly for all that You want to give me today
and help me to receive it with gratitude.*

January 15

In all your dealings, treat others as you would have them treat
you, for this is the sum of biblical teaching.
Gospel Q 16

The Dalai Lama, a great contemporary exponent of
Buddhism, has said that his religion is kindness. Jesus
seems to agree, interpreting his own Jewish scriptural
tradition in terms of the "Golden Rule" that is found in all
the great spiritual paths.

Daily Prayer

***Let me live by this one rule today: that I treat others as I
would like them to treat me.***

January 16

Foxes have dens and birds have nests but I have nowhere
to lay my head.
Matthew 8:20

Jesus walked the earth as a homeless vagrant and identified
his disciples by their concern for the most marginalized
people in the community. It's such a simple criterion and
yet one so easily forgotten.

Daily Prayer

*Help me to be especially attentive to You today in those who
have so little of the world's wealth.*

January 17

Do not fear those who kill the body but cannot touch the
essence of what you are; be afraid of what destroys both your
body and your essential identity.
Gospel Q 46

It has been said that we are not truly alive unless there is
something for which we are ready to die. This implies that
our life contains something more important than our self-
ish ego agenda, something that both defines and challenges
our deepest reality.

Daily Prayer

*Help me to face my fears today, trusting Your love that is
always with me.*

January 18

I thank you, Heavenly Parent, because you have hidden these things from the wise and clever while revealing them to the childlike.
Gospel Q 32

Intellectual ability and education do not automatically translate into a receptivity to the divine and a sensitivity to the ways of the spirit. As the Sufi poet and mystic Rumi says, "Sell your cleverness and buy bewilderment."

Daily Prayer

Help me not to trip on my own cleverness today but rather to keep the openness of a child.

January 19

You know the lay of the land and can read the face of the sky.
So why can't you interpret the here and now?
Gospel Q 59

We gain increasing mastery over nature but can we discern
as skillfully the subtle movements of God's Spirit? The poet
Theodore Roethke exclaims, "O to be delivered from the
rational into the realm of pure song...."

Daily Prayer

Help me to stay attentive to Your will in the world today.

January 20

A shepherd, losing one of his flock of one hundred, will leave the ninety-nine and look for that lost sheep. When he finds it, he'll rejoice, calling out to his friends and neighbors, "Let's celebrate! I've found the sheep that was lost."
Gospel Q 71

God's love is particularly intense for those at risk, for their need is greater. We're called to imitate this divine quality, not running away from "the harder cases" that cross our path.

Daily Prayer

Help me to turn my attention today to those people and situations that most need me, not those that most flatter my ego.

January 21

The God of Abraham, Isaac, and Jacob is a God of the living,
not a God of the dead.
Matthew 22:31-32

Death is the opposite of birth, not of life. Life is changed, not
taken away, when we die. Our metaphors of resurrection and
reincarnation are nothing more than our human attempts to
grasp this mystery. Our challenge is always to choose life.

Daily Prayer

*I thank You that You have chosen me to live forever with
all Your angels and saints.*

January 22

Put your sword back where it belongs, for everyone who takes
up the sword will perish by the sword.
Matthew 26:52

It is a terrible human truth—violence begets more violence. There are so many places in our world where we see
"adults" caught in a deadly cycle of revenge. It is only by
responding to violence with truth, dialogue, and love that
these cycles can be broken.

Daily Prayer

***Help me to break and end any cycles of violence that
entangle me today.***

January 23

You erect monuments to prophets who were murdered by your ancestors. They did the killing, you built the tombs.
Gospel Q 44

Do the schools and streets named after Martin Luther King, Jr., really mean that the racism he condemned has disappeared from our society? The mere change of names doesn't eliminate the work that still has to be done.

Daily Prayer

Help me to focus on the work to be done today and not on congratulating myself for what I did yesterday.

January 24

When you give to charity, don't let your left hand know what
your right hand is doing.
Matthew 6:3

If our gifts have a hook—some expectation of a certain
response or return—they are not true gifts. Giving is a
wonderful practice if it really is a letting go, a total
detachment, a true gift to the other.

Daily Prayer

*Help me to offer true gifts today, to give without agendas
or expectations.*

January 25

I am giving you a new commandment: love one another as
I have loved you.
John 13:34

This commandment is the foundation stone of a practice
which essentially means the effort to live and love as Jesus
did, bringing his perspective to every moral choice, to
every challenging moment along our path.

Daily Prayer

*Help me in the challenging moments of this day to imagine
how Jesus would speak and act, letting that be a guide to
what I say and do.*

January 26

Peace is what I leave behind for you; I give you my peace.
John 14:27

The peace Jesus refers to here is not complacency, the apathy of the uninvolved, but a deep harmony with the divine mystery, the Tao or flow of the universe. Touched by the divine, petty troubles and cares fade away.

Daily Prayer

Thank You for letting me experience Your peace in all the unrest of this day.

January 27

Become passersby.
Gospel of Thomas 42

The Buddha taught: "All that you have, you will lose." Jesus too reminds us that all things pass away and that there is no point in trying to cling to them. Not clinging frees us up to love and cherish what is offered in each moment.

Daily Prayer

Let me experience the deep peace that comes from celebrating what is in each moment without clinging to any of it.

January 28

He who knows all but fails to know himself lacks everything.
Gospel of Thomas 67

Knowledge of things outside of ourselves cannot replace the
inner wisdom that connects us with both our deepest self and
the divine. To act in the world without any effort to clarify
our own consciousness is to court disaster.

Daily Prayer

*May I never confuse worldly knowledge with
spiritual wisdom.*

January 29

Become better than me; be children of the Holy Spirit.
Secret Book of James 5:6

Jesus challenges us to outdo rather than worship him. Every good teacher wants to be surpassed by his or her students. To be led by the divine spirit is to be let loose, not caged.

Daily Prayer

On this day may I burst forth in the power of Your Spirit.

January 30

The only place lacking the truth is any place
where I am absent.
Dialogue of the Savior 24:3-4

Jesus is understood here as God's self-expression, God's
word translating the divine mystery into human words and
deeds. To know the spirit of Jesus and of his teachings is to
know the heart of God.

Daily Prayer

*May I not stray far from Your truth today but may I rather
be where You are.*

January 31

Is it healthy people who need a doctor or the sick? I didn't
come to call the God-centered but the sinners.
Mark 2:17

Like the Buddha, Jesus helped people become whole. But it
was only to the extent that they recognized the need for healing that they could achieve this wholeness. We have to have
the wisdom to know where we hurt.

Daily Prayer

*Heal in me whatever needs to be made whole: my body,
my mind, or my soul.*

February 1

No one patches an old garment with a new and unshrunken
piece of cloth; the new material would rip away from the old
and the garment would be torn more than it was.
Mark 2:21

Jesus' message challenges all existing organizations and
structures; it can't simply be patched on to the status quo,
not even a status quo that bears his name. What he's calling
for is continual renewal. Ecclesia semper reformanda...
the Church always needs to be reformed. So too does every
human heart.

Daily Prayer

*Send forth Your Spirit so that we may be renewed,
reformed, and re-created today.*

February 2

Why are you afraid? Have you still no faith?
Mark 4:40

Our fear stems from a lack of trust in the God who loves us more than we love ourselves. Again and again we find that it is fear alone that blocks our path to healing and wholeness.

Daily Prayer

Grant us a growing trust in You, a faith that will overcome all fear this day.

February 3

Why does this generation ask for a sign? Believe me,
no signs will be given.
Mark 8:15

People of every generation crave to know the future; and yet
the greatest revelation of the divine is always in the present.
A miracle, after all, is not an unusual event but an event to
which we pay unusual attention.

Daily Prayer

*Let me not be distracted or misguided today in looking for
what is unusual and special; rather let me find You and
Your will in the ordinariness of every moment.*

February 4

What does it profit us to gain the whole world while losing
what we most deeply are?
Mark 8:36

Are we, like Esau (Genesis 27), ready to sell our birthright
for a bowl of stew or our soul for a salary? We underestimate
human worth when we rank people by their annual income
or think that material possessions can substitute for a
spiritual life.

Daily Prayer

*Help me today to keep my priorities straight: God first,
God last, God always.*

February 5

Many who are first will be last and the last first.
Mark 10:31

The measure of a person's success by society's standards often does not correspond to God's estimate of that person's excellence. Neither bishop nor CEO wears the mantle of God's privilege. God lines us up by a different measure.

Daily Prayer

Don't let me measure myself and others by society's standards; help me rather to see the world more as You see it.

February 6

Some kinds of demons can be expelled only through prayer.
Mark 9:29

When we believe that only money talks and only chief
executives have clout, the primacy and power of prayer are
easily forgotten. Jesus, however, views prayer as the single
most powerful weapon against the forces of evil in our world.
Prayer not only changes the world; more importantly, it
changes us.

Daily Prayer

*Let me take seriously my vocation to be a person of prayer;
let me not forget that prayer matters and that my prayers
are part of Your Providence.*

February 7

Do you see these magnificent buildings? They will all be
destroyed and not one stone will be left on another.
Mark 13:2

As Jeremiah prophesied the destruction of the First Temple in
587 BCE, so Jesus declares that the Second Temple too will be
destroyed (something that did in fact happen in 70 CE, just
forty years after Jesus' execution by the Romans) unless people
stop placating Caesar and align themselves with God. Only
what is founded on God can last.

Daily Prayer

*Let me not spend my energies today on the passing show of
this world but let me be poured out in service to Your will.*

February 8

If someone wants to sue you for your coat, give him
your shirt as well.
Matthew 5:40

Surrendering both articles of clothing to the rapacious land
owner leaves the peasant farmer naked. One is reminded of the
prophet Isaiah walking around Jerusalem naked for three years
as a sign of the injustice in the land. This kind of unexpected
and counter-intuitive response might prove to be an effective
prophetic sign. On the other hand, it might simply leave us
with neither coat nor shirt and that's OK too.

Daily Prayer

*Don't let me cling to the passing goods of this life; let me
rather stay focused on loving all others unconditionally.*

February 9

Don't store up for yourselves treasure on earth where moth
and rust destroy things and thieves steal them.
Gospel Q 54

The Buddha taught that all things are on fire. We can't
successfully cling to anything earthly nor can we preserve
any kind of worldly treasure since the very nature of everything around us is impermanence. The only solid thing to
hang on to is God's will.

Daily Prayer

*May my storehouse be filled today with
Your reality and love.*

February 10

Why do you notice the speck of sawdust in your neighbor's
eye but fail to see the log in your own?
Gospel Q 20

What annoys us in others is often a small version of what
exists on a larger scale in ourselves. Why is it always so much
more attractive to do our neighbor's practice rather than to do
our own? We are all human, all imperfect.

Daily Prayer

*Help me to look at others today with compassion and to
direct my critical tendencies to my own practice.*

February 11

Enter through the narrow gate, for the gate is wide and the road is easy leading to destruction and there are many who take it.
Gospel Q 63

This passage is not about condemning a lot of people to hell. It is a reminder that a narrow gate is entered single file, for each of our spiritual paths is unique. The wide gate, however, admits a crowd where individuals and their spirituality are inevitably lost. Enlightenment happens one person at a time.

Daily Prayer

Help me to walk the unique path to which You call me, not the smooth path of "mega-church salvation."

February 12

Take neither wallet nor bag, neither a change of clothes
or sandals.
Gospel Q 29

Nothing could challenge a consumer society more than such a
radical teaching of poverty, detachment, and total dependence
on God and the good will of others. This is a teaching we are
understandably hesitant to hear.

Daily Prayer

*If I don't walk literally among the homeless today,
let me at least be homeless at heart, knowing that
my true home is in Your will.*

February 13

As you enter a house, greet it. If the house deserves your message, let your peace come upon it; if not, your peace will return to you.
Gospel Q 30

We see here the near-physical character in words of greeting, blessing, and curse within the ancient Jewish tradition. Receptivity is crucial or even the gift of peace is sent back unopened.

Daily Prayer

Let me greet with peace every house I enter today.

February 14

A student is not above the teacher nor a servant above the master. It is enough for a student to be like the teacher and the servant to be like the master.
Matthew 10:24

There's no need to try to be better than anyone; Jesus wants to eliminate every kind of elitism. Where teachers, students, servants, and masters are alike, the categories lose their rigidity and we realize that we really are all brothers and sisters.

Daily Prayer

Let me not spend today climbing the ladder that puts me above people but joining the circle where we are all equal in Your eyes.

February 15

Do not think that I have come to bring peace; I have come to
bring a sword of division.
Gospel Q 57

Jesus comes, not to placate, but to challenge. His teachings, like the sharpest of swords, cut through the phony
distinctions we make between deserving and undeserving
poor, between successful people and failures, between
first- and second-class citizens, between first-world and
third-world countries.

Daily Prayer

*I will strive to be a peacemaker today but not at the price of
accepting injustice.*

February 16

I have come to set a man against his father, a daughter against her mother, a daughter-in-law against her mother-in-law; one's enemies will be members of one's own household.
Gospel Q 57

The three examples attack the conventional patriarchal lines of authority. One's allegiances should not be to any system in which some people are more important than others, since all are equal before God. All elitist structures are necessarily false.

Daily Prayer

Let me help dismantle all systems of inequality, since any privileging of one group over another insults God's role as our only true Parent.

February 17

On the day of judgment you will have to give an account for
every careless word you utter.
Matthew 12:36

Words can hurt or heal, encourage or drive to despair,
enlighten or confuse. Words bear consequences that merit our
respect. The Letter of James (chapter three) reminds us of the
difficulty of subduing our tongue.

Daily Prayer

Let me speak with care and compassion today.

February 18

When an unclean spirit finds as empty house, it brings
along seven other spirits more evil than itself and they
enter and live there.
Gospel Q 39

Nature abhors a vacuum and so too does the spiritual life.
The best way to displace evil is for our hearts to be filled with
what is positive, good, and life-enhancing.

Daily Prayer

**Let there be no space in me where You are not present, no
corner of my life which You do not fill.**

February 19

If one of your circle offends you, go and point out the fault
when the two of you are alone.
Gospel Q 77

Public shaming of others is strongly condemned in the Jewish
ethical tradition, which Jesus affirms in this saying. To embar-
rass others, even when trying to communicate constructive
criticism, ends up hurting more than helping them.

Daily Prayer

*If I need to criticize someone today, let me make sure that it
is in a context that is private and respectful of that person's
feelings.*

February 20

All who puff themselves up will be brought low, while the
humble will be exalted.
Gospel Q 67

One of the many paradoxes of spiritual life and growth is that
our grasping for position or rank reveals how far behind we
really are. Even wanting enlightenment betrays our spiritual
immaturity. For when enlightenment comes, there is no one
there to be enlightened. Why? Because the false self
(the egoic self) will have been dissolved by then into the
authentic self, the God-centered self.

Daily Prayer

*Help me live my life today realizing that I need no external
label or status to confirm my true worth in Your eyes.*

February 21

Damn you, religious hypocrites, white-washed tombs, full of
dead people's bones. You look God-centered on the outside
but inside you are full of hypocrisy.
Matthew 23:27-28

Representatives of religion are especially vulnerable to denying their shadows in an effort to better play their expected
roles in society. This unrealistic expectation leads both to
personal tragedy and to the painful abuse of innocent people,
especially children, who are so tenderly loved by God.

Daily Prayer

*Let what I say and do today be a true reflection of what is
in my heart.*

February 22

Love your brother like your soul; guard him like the
apple of your eye.
Gospel of Thomas 25

Those who share our spiritual quest should be our dearest
friends. St. Augustine wrote that a good friend is "half of our
soul." Our friends are special blessings from God, providing
the soil where we best grow to that fullness of life to which
we are called.

Daily Prayer

*Let me be grateful today for the friends I have and open to
the new friends I may find along my path.*

February 23

I came to set the earth on fire and how I wish it were
already ablaze.
Luke 12:49

The words and teachings of Jesus are not all easy to hear; they
often threaten to destroy what we've come to trust: property
and status, for example, or prestige and power. The fire Jesus
speaks of here is a cleansing fire filled with God's spirit.

Daily Prayer

*Today I will honestly try to surrender myself and all that is
mine to Your transforming fire.*

February 24

I am the light that is above everything, I am all; all came
forth from me and all has returned to me. Split the wood and I
am there. Lift up the stone and you will find me there.
Gospel of Thomas 77

These are striking metaphors for the closeness of the divine; it
brushes against us in every moment of every day but often we
lack the eyes to see, the ears to listen.

Daily Prayer

*Let me live my life today with that extra moment of
awareness that allows me to see Your mystery beneath
the play of all created things.*

February 25

Damn those who require an intercessor or stand in need of
grace and congratulations to those who stand on their own
feet and obtain grace for themselves.
Secret Book of James 7:2-3

A strong condemnation of the kind of religion that focuses on
worshiping Jesus instead of following him, fixating on what
he did or can do instead of heeding his call to a spirituality of
personal transformation and responsibility.

Daily Prayer

Let me never use Your love as an excuse for my own apathy.

February 26

To those who have, more will be given; from those who have not, even what they have will be taken away.
Mark 4:25

Growth in virtue is exponential; so too is growth in vice. Each step we take facilitates future steps in the same direction; each door we open makes it possible to open others of the same kind.

Daily Prayer

Let every step I take today be along the path of Your will; let every door I open lead to You.

February 27

The child is sleeping, not dead. Get up, little girl.
Mark 5:39 & 41

Death doesn't have the finality for Jesus that it does in our
more limited view. For the great spiritual teachers, death is
the opposite of birth, not of life. In the words of the old Latin
Mass for the dead, Vita mutatur, non tollitur: life is changed,
not taken away.

Daily Prayer

*Help me to trust Your power to overcome the finality of all
the earth's deaths.*

February 28

Take courage; I'm here; don't be afraid.
Mark 6:50

God reveals himself to Moses as the one who will be with those who are oppressed and victimized. God is the great WITH of human experience, closer to us than we are to ourselves. As the Koran reminds us, God is closer to us than our jugular!

Daily Prayer

Thank You for encompassing me with Your presence, Your power, and Your compassion.

February 29 (Leap Year)

Whoever wants to be first must be last and servant of all.
Mark 9:35

Spiritual power does not consist of lording it over others
or manipulating them but in facilitating their growth and
life. So much of the power exercised in families, countries,
and religious institutions is egotistic manipulation and
dominance.

Daily Prayer

Let me empower people today, not overpower them.

March 1

Whoever does not receive God's reign as a little child will
never enter it.
Mark 10:15

The spiritual life becomes available to us only if we are as
open and fresh to learn as little children. They meet the world
without the overlay of prejudicial grids we build up by the
time we're adults. In Buddhism this is called
"beginner's mind."

Daily Prayer

*Help me to see everything in Your world today with fresh
eyes and to hear everything with new ears.*

March 2

Why do you call me good? No one is good but God alone.
Mark 10:18

Jesus did not point people to himself but to God. Our worship of Jesus may well be our worst disservice to him and the easiest way of effectively ignoring him. The religion about Jesus is quite different from the religion of Jesus.

Daily Prayer

May my honoring Jesus never stand in the way of the more important challenge to imitate him in his openness to the divine.

March 3

A camel can more easily fit through the eye of a needle than a rich person into God's reign.
Mark 10:25

Attachment and clinging to the goods and goals of worldly life—not the goods and goals themselves—close us to God's purposes and plans. We can have only one highest priority. Will it be our portfolio, our Porsche, or God?

Daily Prayer

Don't let anything I have distract me from the life to which You call me.

March 4

God is God of the living, not of the dead.
Mark 12:27

Is death the opposite of life? Then death is the end. Is death the opposite of birth? Then death is a bridge. Life is changed when we die, not taken away. There really is a "communion of saints" and we are called to that company.

Daily Prayer

Let me remember today that I don't live my life alone but am encouraged and supported by all who have walked in faith and passed on before me.

March 5

Heaven and earth will pass away but my words will not
pass away.
Mark 17:31

The teachings of Jesus transcend this world, stemming as they
do from the heart of the divine mystery. Their truth, therefore, does not pass away with the dissolution of the physical
universe.

Daily Prayer

*Let Your words, not the chatter of the talk shows, guide my
life and choices today.*

March 6

No one knows the day or hour of the end times, not the angels in heaven, not even the Son, but only our Heavenly Parent.
Mark 13:32

Countless people today seem preoccupied with the end of the world countdown. They are concerned that they not be "left behind" when Jesus comes on the clouds. Jesus, however, claimed no knowledge of this entire business and had even less interest in it. True religion always lies in our response and openness to the here and now.

Daily Prayer

Don't let me be sidetracked by worrying about an unknowable future; let me rather center on the knowable here and now with its transparent invitation to life.

March 7

It is a blessing to be meek; you will inherit the earth.
Gospel Q 11

Meekness is not weakness. It suggests a gentleness of spirit, an openness and receptivity to others. We cannot truly learn from others or from life unless we have space, room in ourselves to receive. The Chinese saying reminds us that the ocean is the greatest body of waters because it lies the lowest and can thus receive all the waters of the earth.

Daily Prayer

Let me be consciously meek and strong today, not arrogant and weak.

March 8

Until heaven and earth pass away, not one letter, not one comma will be taken from the Torah until all is fulfilled.
Gospel Q 74

Jesus did not come to reject or replace his own Judaism with another religion. Its basic revelation (the Torah, the first five books of the Bible) and its covenant with God remain valid until the completion of human history, when all religions become obsolete.

Daily Prayer

Let me live Your word today for Your word contains eternal life.

March 9

Seek first God's reign and a life centered in God; all the other things you need will be given to you then as well.
Gospel Q 53

What are our priorities? If God's will is first on the list, everything else will find its proper order and place. We are reminded once again that we cannot have more than one highest priority or ultimate concern, just as we cannot have more than one God.

Daily Prayer

Don't let me lose sight of You and Your will in the busy-ness of this day.

March 10

God's reign is close at hand. Cure the sick, raise the dead, heal
the lepers, cast out demons.
Matthew 10:7 & 8a

God's reign is close at hand because it is available to us as
power. The magnitude of this transformative power boggles
the mind and breaks all the parameters of conventional
wisdom's expectations.

Daily Prayer

*Let my presence be a healing one for all those
I encounter today.*

March 11

Nothing is covered up that will not be uncovered and nothing secret will remain unknown.
Gospel Q 45

Every injustice and hidden sin will be revealed, as will every kind word and deed. Truth is the only democracy. Nothing can be isolated from the whole fabric of society and indeed of reality itself. We belong to the universe in each of our words and actions.

Daily Prayer

Let me realize in all my words and deeds today that all our choices are made under the eye of heaven.

March 12

If it is by the spirit of God that I cast out demons, then the
reign of God has come to you.
Matthew 12:28

"Satan" means "hinderer" or "obstacle." Satan's reign is
opposed to God's reign because it enslaves people, whereas
God's reign liberates. The liberation of people from the
demons of fear, despair, and guilt are signs
of God's presence.

Daily Prayer

*Let nothing that I do today hinder Your reign; rather, let
my every word and deed bring freedom to others at every
level of their life experience.*

March 13

God's reign is like yeast that a woman put in fifty pounds of
flour until the whole mass of dough was leavened.
Gospel Q 62

Life surrounds us with a lot of heavy dough, the stuff of our
daily lives. Only the presence and the power of the divine
spirit can cause it to rise and eventually become edible bread,
something by which others can be nourished.

Daily Prayer

*May the dough of my day rise into a wonderful loaf of bread
that can feed both myself and others.*

March 14

Watch out for those who take the money of the poor under
religious pretenses; their sentence will be all the heavier.
Luke 20:47

Any funds collected in the name of religion must scrupulously
be monitored so that it is truly the disadvantaged who are
helped by them. There are no monies for which human beings
will be held more accountable.

Daily Prayer

*Help me to be vigilant in making sure that any monies
collected through religious organizations with which I am
affiliated go directly to the needy.*

March 15

God's reign is like a merchant in search of beautiful pearls.
Finding a truly priceless pearl, the merchant sells
everything else to buy it.
Matthew 13:45

To be deeply in love stands worlds apart from addictive code-
pendency, just as being centered in the divine mystery exceeds
any comparison with material possessions. If we realized this,
it would be much easier not to cling to what is passing.

Daily Prayer

*Help me in each moment of this day to find the priceless
pearl of Your will and Your reign.*

March 16

Every Torah scholar trained in God's reign is like a steward who brings from his storehouse treasures old and new.
Matthew 13:52

The great wisdom traditions reach back to the beginning of human experience and yet they offer fresh insight for living our lives today. Their wisdom is more contemporary than the latest fashion, fad, or headline.

Daily Prayer

Let all I do today be motivated not by the latest slogans and fads but by Your deep and everlasting wisdom.

March 17

By your endurance you will gain your souls.
Luke 21:19

Beginning a task is easy; perseverance is a more challenging matter, especially when opposition arises and hindrances appear on every side. And yet, it is precisely such challenges that separate God's true disciples from mere camp followers.

Daily Prayer

Help me to persevere in Your service, especially in those areas where I experience the most opposition.

March 18

The night is coming when no one can work. As long as I am
in the world, I am its light.
John 9:4

We have to walk with the light we have with every step we
take along our way to the divine center. There is always a step
to be taken and always a light shining to illuminate that step.

Daily Prayer

*Let me follow Your lead and Your light in every step
I take this day.*

March 19

There are many mansions in my Heavenly Parent's home.
John 14:2

What a challenge this verse presents to every form of religious exclusivism. There is no one way, no single truth for everyone that we can display as a bumper sticker or hold up on a sign at a football game. God's love offers a home to the human family in all its diversity.

Daily Prayer

Let me celebrate today the magnificent inclusiveness of Your love by making room in my heart for all my brothers and sisters in all their rich diversity.

March 20

I am the way, the truth, and the life. No one comes to the
Heavenly Parent except through me.
John 14:6

Peoples of every religion, as well as those with none, come to
the divine only through the receptive child-parent consciousness so clearly manifested in Jesus' life.
This teaching has nothing to do with requiring people to
become Christians to be saved or made whole. It doesn't close
doors but opens them.

Daily Prayer

*Thank You for letting me trust you this day as a child trusts
a loving parent.*

March 21

I promise you that you won't enter heaven's reign through my
decision but because you yourselves are full.
Secret Book of James 2:6

An empowering statement, asking us not to rely on Jesus to
do those things for us which we have to grow up and learn to
do for ourselves. Jesus' teachings never limit our autonomy
but instead reveal to us our staggering potential.

Daily Prayer

*Thank You for filling me with Your life, Your love, and
Your power this day.*

March 22

We were not made for the Sabbath; the Sabbath was
made for us.
Mark 2:27

All religions, with all their rites and rules, are but vehicles to
help us on our way to God. It is a perversion when the means
becomes the end. Religions, after all, are created by human
beings, whereas reality is created by God.

Daily Prayer

*Thank You for giving me in the many religions of the world
vehicles to link me to Your life and Your will.*

March 23

Go home to your friends and tell them how much the Lord
has done for you.
Mark 5:19

The fullness of every moment comes from God's hand. Instead
of complaining, we should rejoice in life's gifts, sharing with
others the divine love that enriches us from day to day. The
spirit of complaining kills the spirit of thanksgiving.

Daily Prayer

*Thank You for all the circumstances of this day; help me to
see each moment as an opportunity to love and serve You.*

March 24

Prophets are not without honor, except in their hometowns,
among their own relations, and in their own house.
Mark 6:4

Rushing to hear the guest lecturer from the distant city, we
often ignore the truth we could learn from those who are closest to us. By despising the familiar and seeking out the exotic,
we often miss the truth we need to hear.

Daily Prayer

***Keep me alert today to learn from those who are
nearest to me.***

March 25

You abandon the commandments of God and cling to
human traditions.
Mark 7:8

Religions all too readily fall into idolatry, worshipping their
own practices and precepts, instead of the divine reality to
which they should be pointing. God's will then becomes sub-
ordinated to our human preferences and predilections.

Daily Prayer

*Let me always remember that religion is the vehicle but
You are the goal, religion is the striving but You are what is
complete.*

March 26

There is nothing outside of us that defiles us by entering
our bodies but the things that come out of us can
definitely be defiling.
Mark 7:15

Our spiritual health is more affected by what we think and say
than by what we eat and drink. The prideful thoughts we have
while abstaining from meat harm us more than ever the meat
could. After all, the Dalai Lama eats meat, whereas Hitler was
a strict vegetarian.

Daily Prayer

*Let me always be more attentive to what is in my heart
than to what is in my refrigerator, to what is on my mind
more than to what is on my plate.*

March 27

Do you have eyes and fail to see? Do you have ears and
fail to hear?
Mark 8:18

Hearing is not the same as listening nor does seeing necessarily entail being aware. Receptivity is the key to any kind of
understanding. We must keep ourselves open and create those
spaces of silence where we make room for God.

Daily Prayer

*May the eyes of my eyes and the ears of my ears
be open today.*

March 28

Whoever welcomes a child in my name welcomes me and whoever welcomes me welcomes the one who sent me.
Mark 9:37

We're so careful to pay attention to "important" people and often neglect those who aren't well dressed, affluent, physically attractive, or societally powerful. We can miss a lot of God's children this way.

Daily Prayer

Today may I see the divine image in those I meet who are without power or prestige, without wealth or charm.

March 29

Give to Caesar the coins that bear his image but give to God
the human beings created in the divine image.
Mark 12:17

This is not a command to pay taxes but a teaching about
our divine identity. Jesus doesn't really care what happens to
the coins that bear Caesar's image but he cares deeply that
we who bear God's image be given totally to God's will and
God's reign.

Daily Prayer

*I am grateful to be made in the divine image and I pray
that I reflect God in all that I say and do this day.*

March 30

This is my body; this is my blood of the covenant.
Mark 14:24

Jesus identifies himself with the broken bread and the poured
out wine at a Passover Seder, his last meal with his friends.
His last days set the seal to his whole life of service to others.
He was indeed obedient to God's word, even as he entered the
jaws of death.

Daily Prayer

Let me recognize You wherever a life is broken in Your
service, wherever a person is poured out in Your love.

March 31

It is a blessing to be compassionate; you will receive
compassion.
Gospel Q 12

This asks for more than pity. It includes an ability to empa-
thize, to get inside the pain of another, and to act from that
point of identification. "Compassion" means feeling with
the other.

Daily Prayer

**Don't let me meet others today in a pitying or patronizing
way but with true love and compassion.**

April 1

It is a blessing to be among the peacemakers; you will be called God's children.
Gospel Q 12

The prophet Isaiah tells us (Isaiah 32) that peace is the result of justice and God-centeredness. It is by praying for and working towards a just and God-centered home, workplace, neighborhood, nation, and world that we are peacemakers.

Daily Prayer

Help me to keep my ears open to the call of justice, so that I may lay the groundwork for true peace.

April 2

When you are offering your gift at the altar and remember
a quarrel with a neighbor, leave your gift and go first to be
reconciled with your neighbor and then come back to offer
your gift.
Matthew 5:23

The rites and rules of religion are always to be regarded as
secondary and subordinate to the demands of reality. As Franz
Rosenzweig, a Jewish philosopher and religious thinker, said:
"God didn't create religion after all but reality."

Daily Prayer

*Help me to remember today that missing a religious
ritual is of less importance to God than missing a
neighbor in need.*

April 3

Give to everyone who begs from you and don't refuse anyone
who wants to borrow from you.
Matthew 5:42

Nothing really belongs to us; we are only stewards for what
belongs to God. In Psalm 24 we read that "The earth is the
Lord's and all that is in it." And in Leviticus 25:23 we are told
by God, "No land may be sold outright, because the land is
mine, and you come to it as aliens and tenants of mine." These
texts should lead us to lives of generosity rather than of
calculation and greed.

Daily Prayer

*Help me to live this day with a generous heart, remember-
ing that everything I have is on loan from You.*

April 4

Be perfect as your Heavenly Parent is perfect.
Gospel Q 17

We are called to come to our fullness, just as God is fully all
that God can be. Our perfection is to be awake, God-centered,
and without the burden of any fear or anxiety. To be perfect is
not to be without flaw but fully to be.

Daily Prayer

*Let me be stretched today so that I may more totally embrace
the life and the love to which You call me.*

April 5

You should never be joyful, except when you are looking at
your brothers and sisters with love.
Gospel of the Hebrews 5

It's a profound realization that we can't be truly joyful if
we are isolated from the love that should always be our
bond to our fellow human beings. Any joy not based on
such love is superficial and unreal. At best, it is narcissism;
at worst, it is sin.

Daily Prayer

*Let me find joy today in the love I experience in community
with my brothers and sisters, Your children.*

April 6

When you pray, don't heap up empty phrases like people who think they'll be heard because of their many words. Don't be like them, for your Heavenly Parent knows what you need before you ask.

Matthew 6:7

Prayer is not something to impress or inform God. It is a way of being with God and of co-creating the world God wants to call into being. Our prayer should be simple and sincere, filled with a great trust.

Daily Prayer

Let the prayers of my lips today be but a reflection of the deepest prayers of my heart.

April 7

When you fast, wash and groom yourself so that your fasting
may be seen, not by others, but by your Heavenly Parent.
Matthew 6:18

Like all religious activities, fasting should be a practice to
facilitate our relationship with God, not something done to
impress others. It also allows us to feel need and to experience
openness, helping us to identify with our many sisters and
brothers who live without food by circumstance and not by
the luxury of choice provided by a voluntary fast.

Daily Prayer

Let my fasting be a vehicle to You, not a pious show.

April 8

The eye is the lamp of the body. So if your eye is healthy, your whole body will be full of light.
Matthew 6:22

The Hindus regard the third eye (invisibly located in the middle of the forehead) as the sixth chakra or energy center, the site of spiritual wisdom and a source of light. It is this single eye that Jesus identifies as the lamp of the body.

Daily Prayer

Let my spiritual eye be healthy today so that my whole being may be full of Your light.

April 9

No one can serve two masters; you cannot serve
God and money.
Matthew 6:24

It's not that we can't have money but that we can't worship it
while claiming to worship God. As Rabbi Abraham Joshua
Heschel said, "God must either be of supreme importance or
of no importance at all."

Daily Prayer

*Let my life be poured out in Your service today, tolerating
no rival to You.*

April 10

Don't judge so that you yourself will not be judged.
Matthew 7:1

We are simply not in a position ever to know the inner relationship of another human being to God. We can judge
external behavior and deal with it as we have to but the inner
standing of another person before God is simply not our
business. The Buddhists remind us not to waste our time on
anyone else's practice.

Daily Prayer

*Keep me from judging others today. If I must judge, let me
judge myself.*

April 11

Beware of false prophets who come to you dressed like sheep
but inside are hungry wolves.
Matthew 7:15

Religious scam artists thrive in every generation. Their hunger for power and money exposes their falseness, no matter how flashy their robes and rings. Ignore their rhetoric and pay attention to what they're doing for the poor and marginalized.

Daily Prayer

Let everything I do in the name of religion today be for Your glory and for the good of my neighbor.

April 12

Follow me and let the dead bury the dead.
Gospel Q 27

The past is dead. A spiritual life focuses on the here and now, the present moment that alone is real and always adequate for practice. We have to run to stay up with spiritual adepts like Jesus; our rationalizations and excuses are merely stumbling blocks.

Daily Prayer

Don't let me be caught up in the past today for it is only in the present moment that I can hear and respond to the divine call.

April 13

The harvest is ready but the workers are few.
Matthew 9:37

Martin Buber, a great Jewish religious thinker, urged all the religions to reach out to the spiritually homeless. This does not include trying to convert people from one spiritual home to another; such efforts are of the ego alone.

Daily Prayer

Let my life with others today be a witness to Your existence and to Your reign.

April 14

I am sending you out like sheep among wolves, so be wise as
serpents and innocent as doves.
Matthew 10:16

We are not encouraged to be naive about the ways of the
world; we need to employ skilled strategies that are effective
in transforming our world. Wisdom and innocence can indeed
be combined.

Daily Prayer

*Let me use all available knowledge and skill today in the
accomplishment of Your will in the world.*

April 15

What I say to you in the dark, tell in the light; and what you hear whispered, shout from the house top.
Matthew 10:27

There is a Buddhist saying that there are no secret teachings, only secret ears. The truth is for everyone but it needs to be proclaimed by our lives, not only by our lips.

Daily Prayer

Let me proclaim Your good news in all that I say and do today.

April 16

All things have been handed over to me by my Heavenly Parent and no one knows the Child except the Parent, just as no one knows the Parent except the Child.
Gospel Q 32

Whether we are Hindu or Buddhist, Jewish or Christian, with or without religious affiliation, we can be intimate with the divine reality only by being in the receptive stance of child to parent embodied so perfectly by Jesus.

Daily Prayer

Let me do all things with You today and nothing without You.

April 17

Whoever does the will of God is my brother and sister
and mother.
Mark 3:35

The real relatives of Jesus are not those who share his blood
but those who unite with him in his pursuit of God's will.
True discipleship makes us a contemporary of Jesus, a com-
panion in his work, a member of his family.

Daily Prayer

*Thank You for allowing me to be a member of Jesus' true
family by challenging me to do Your will.*

April 18

If two of you on earth agree on anything you ask for, it will be done for you by my Heavenly Parent.
Matthew 18:19

There's power in numbers, even when it comes to prayer. We are encouraged to pray with others, forming a community of prayer like the minyan required for a synagogue service. Such a community manifests God's reign.

Daily Prayer

Thank You for allowing me to participate in the communion of saints, the prayerful community of those who seek to do Your will.

April 19

Take care that you do not despise one of these little ones, for their angels continually see the face of my Heavenly Parent.
Matthew 18:10

Sin against the neighbor is always an offense against God but much more so when the neighbor has less power, less life experience, and fewer resources. Disparity of power all too easily provides an inroad for harassment or assault. Abuse of children brings tears to God's eyes.

Daily Prayer

Let me be an advocate today for all children and for all those people society judges to be without importance, consequence, or value.

April 20

Call no one on earth your father, for you have one
Father—the one in heaven.
Matthew 23:9

This represents a strong blow to patriarchy, the conventional
wisdom of Jesus' day and, to a large extent, of ours as well. We
are all brothers and sisters, equal under one Heavenly Parent.
We find arrogance and abuse of power at the top of patriarchy's pyramid and infantalism and lack of self-esteem
at its bottom.

Daily Prayer

*Let me not surrender my responsibility today to anyone
claiming higher authority or standing.*

April 21

Why were you looking for me? Didn't you know that I had to be in my Heavenly Parent's house?
Luke 2:49

Jesus is portrayed here as a twelve-year old who already senses his deep vocation both to experience God as Heavenly Parent and to act as God's child in the world. This is his Bar Mitzvah, his coming of age as a Jew.

Daily Prayer

Help me to live this day as someone called to live in Your house.

April 22

No one who puts his hand to the plow and looks back is ready
for God's reign.
Luke 9:62

It takes courage to choose life and the more focused we are
in that pursuit, the better. A constant going back and forth
impedes our progress. Looking back turned Lot's wife into a
pillar of salt (Genesis 19:26).

Daily Prayer

*Don't let me vacillate in Your service today but keep me
steady and on course.*

April 23

The time is coming—in fact, it is already here—when we will
worship God neither on Mount Gerizim nor on Mount Zion
but in spirit and truth.
John 4:23

No place is closer to God than any other for someone whose
heart is truly open to the divine reality. The receptive heart
is always God's favorite dwelling place, vastly superior to the
most beautiful temple, cathedral, or mosque.

Daily Prayer

Help me to be close to Your heart wherever I am today.

April 24

Let whoever seeks not cease from his seeking until he finds.
When he finds, he will be troubled. When he is troubled, he
will marvel and will reign over all.
Gospel of Thomas 2

The "I found it" bumper sticker is never the final truth; finding is followed by the troubling awareness that the divine
mystery can never be fully found; this in turn leads to a new
sense of awe and finally to the deepest kind of spiritual power.

Daily Prayer

*Don't let me settle today for complacency or easy answers
but keep me growing in Your spirit.*

April 25

Damn you, religious leaders, who load people down with burdens that you don't lift a finger to carry yourselves.
Gospel Q 44

As soon as a religious organization creates a division between us and them, between privileged leaders and lowly followers, between insiders and outsiders, the way to true spiritual growth is impeded.

Daily Prayer

Let me try to meet all others today as brothers and sisters, not as servants or subordinates, inferiors or people of no account.

April 26

His disciples said to him, "On what day will the repose of the dead occur and when does the new world come?" He said to them, "That repose you look for has come, but you have not recognized it."
Gospel of Thomas 51

God's reign does not wait for some future date set in a heavenly calendar; it is here and it is now. We just need to stop, look, and listen! We also need to obey, since God's reign comes where God's will is done "on earth as in heaven."

Daily Prayer

Thank You for surrounding me with the blessings of Your reign.

April 27

...The kingdom of the father is spread out on the earth and
people do not see it.
Gospel of Thomas 113

This is a striking image of the availability of the divine reality. Yet our human resistance prevents us from seeing what
should be most obvious to us. What keeps us from noticing
this Presence spread out before us?

Daily Prayer

*Don't let me miss Your realm today in my preoccupation
with trivial matters and superficial concerns.*

April 28

Which is easier to say, "Your sins are forgiven" or "Pick up
your mat and walk"?
Mark 2:8

Jesus intends to announce that God has forgiven this man's
sins when he is challenged by some of his opponents. He proceeds then to heal the man's physical ailment as well, giving
this teaching to show that for him the human person is one
and every form of healing is holistic.

Daily Prayer

*Keep me whole, healthy, and holy today and let me be an
instrument of healing for others too.*

April 29

Get these things out of here! How dare you use my Heavenly
Parent's house as a market.
John 2:16

Jesus incited a riot in the Temple because closeness to God
was being brokered. The poor were buying sacrificial birds
they could ill afford while the rich led bulls and sheep to the
altar. Affluence should never translate into spiritual worth.

Daily Prayer

*Help me to realize that $100 in the collection plate does not
attract Your attention to my prayers.*

April 30

Your faith has made you well; go in peace.
Mark 5:34

Our potential for being healed stands in direct relationship
to our willingness to trust the divine healer. Healing always
brings inner peace in its wake. We are not always called to be
cured but we are always called to be healed.

Daily Prayer

Trusting in You, my faith is constant.

May 1

Unless the kernel of wheat falls to the earth and
dies, it remains a single seed; but if it dies,
it produces a great harvest.
John 12:24

The cherished ego must shrivel up and die for the pure grain
of the God-centered self to emerge. The "old being" must be
shuffled off so that the "new being" can emerge. What Asian
religions call "the small self" must give way to "the great
self." The false self must dissolve into the authentic self.

Daily Prayer

Don't let me be afraid of losing my false self to You.

May 2

Those who want to be my disciples must deny themselves,
take up their cross, and follow me.
Mark 8:34

The cross is already there for each of us. The only choice is
whether to take it up or try to deny its existence. The cross is
the dukkha of Buddhism's First Noble Truth, the unsatisfac-
tory character of our existence in any moment.

Daily Prayer

*Thank You for helping me both to see and to shoulder the
cross that is on my path today.*

May 3

When you are ready to pray, first let go of anything you are holding against another.
Mark 11:26

We cannot ask God to forgive our failings unless we first forgive those who have failed us. This is not an arbitrary rule on God's part. It is the way reality works. Forgiving others keeps open our channel to God.

Daily Prayer

Don't let me lose contact with You today by turning a brother or sister into an enemy.

May 4

Whatever you ask for in prayer, believe that you have received it, and it will be yours.
Mark 11:24

Prayer is not about cajoling God to give us good things but realizing that God already offers us infinitely more good than we are ready to recognize or receive. God always loves us more than we love ourselves and wants our good more than we do.

Daily Prayer

Thank You for filling my life today with more blessings than I could ever hope for or imagine.

May 5

When you're brought to trial unjustly, say what comes to you
in the moment, confident that it is the Holy Spirit
speaking in you.
Mark 13:11

It is especially in trying times that God is with us, if we can
be open and receptive to the divine presence. We have not
been cast as orphans into the universe. We are never alone if
we allow God into our lives.

Daily Prayer

*Thank You for helping me to realize that nothing can
separate me from You except my own decision to be closed to
Your Spirit.*

May 6

It is a blessing to be poor; God's reign is yours.
Gospel Q 9

Being poor is not a matter of how much money is in our pockets but how much ego is in our hearts. The key to all spiritual growth is receptivity. And emptiness is the prerequisite for receiving the infinite treasure that God has to give.

Daily Prayer

*Keep me poor today so that my emptiness will attract
Your fullness.*

May 7

It is a blessing to mourn; you will be comforted.
Gospel Q 10

To mourn entails a capacity to feel the pain of others and to be compassionate enough to care. We can't feel another's pain unless we create room for compassion in ourselves. We have to be able to step aside from our own ego to truly help others.

Daily Prayer

Let me be able to see beyond my own agenda so that I can feel the pain that is in the brothers and sisters I meet along my way.

May 8

It is a blessing to be persecuted for walking in God's ways;
God's reign is yours.
Matthew 5:10

When we follow God's invitation to love justice and compassion, we may meet resistance from the forces of greed and pride that keep much of the world's population in poverty and misery. Opposition by the entrenched power of wealth and privilege tells us that we're on the right track.

Daily Prayer

Let me not be afraid of the forces in my world today that oppose Your reign of peace and justice.

May 9

If someone strikes you on your right cheek, turn
the other also.
Matthew 5:39

If I'm hit on the right cheek, the aggressor is using the back
of the hand, the way one strikes an inferior. By turning the
other cheek I change the situation, since the second blow will
have to be struck with the full hand or fist, the way one strikes
an equal. We don't love others by letting them disrespect us,
even when superior power is theirs.

Daily Prayer

*Help me to realize today that letting others disrespect me
is a way of failing to love them, since it feeds their illusion
that they alone deserve respect.*

May 10

When you pray, hide yourself in your room, shutting the door,
and then pray to your Heavenly Parent who is a hidden God.
Matthew 6:6

Prayer, like all religious practice, should be something we
do, not for the applause and approval of others, but for
God and for our own growth. Religion as showmanship
insults God and demeans God's people. Unfortunately, as
Chogyam Trungpa once said, "We all want to witness our own
enlightenment."

Daily Prayer

*Let the sincere prayer of my heart be the deepest part of my
life with You.*

May 11

Give without payment what you received without payment.
Matthew 10:8b

We're socialized to a society in which everything and every-one has a price. We suffer from a plague of greed and ego-centeredness. The divine wisdom that invites us to a profound generosity totally subverts our "bottom line" mentality.

Daily Prayer

Don't let me be deluded and driven by the quid pro quo mentality that separates me from You and others.

May 12

Come to me, all you who are weary and carrying heavy burdens, and I will give you rest.
Matthew 11:29

A life apart from some experience of the divine mystery is bound to be burdensome and depressing. Jesus' role was and is to mediate that divine presence and peace.
There is no heavier burden we carry than our own ego with the tangle of neuroses and lies that support it.

Daily Prayer

Let me put down today the burdens my ego creates and accept the rest that only You can provide.

May 13

Take my yoke upon you and learn from me for I am gentle and
humble of heart and you will find rest for your souls.
Matthew 10:29

Authentic spiritual teachings never burden us with guilt and
empty obligation; they rather invite us to growth and fuller
life. Jesus invites; he doesn't threaten or try to generate guilt.

Daily Prayer

*May the gentle and humble heart of Jesus be created
in me today.*

May 14

Be ready to forgive your brother or sister, not seven times but
seventy times seven times.
Gospel Q 77

It's difficult for us to understand the scope of the divine love
and forgiveness we are invited to imitate and manifest. But to
soften our hostile reactions, to breathe deeply and forgive, can
benefit us as much as it helps our relations with others.

Daily Prayer

*Help me to stop counting when it comes to forgiving others,
just as I don't want to count how often I've been forgiven.*

May 15

Heavenly Parent, if it is not possible for this cup to pass without my drinking it, your will be done.
Matthew 26:42

Walking a spiritual path does not mean that we are excited at the prospect of suffering. It does mean trusting the God who is with us even in our suffering and who can help us transform death itself into life.

Daily Prayer

Help me trust Your will today knowing that what it offers me is always love, infinite and abundant love.

May 16

Can one blind person guide another without both of them
falling into the ditch?
Gospel Q 19

It's difficult for us to give advice about what we haven't experienced; in some cases we're better to refer people to those
further along the path than ourselves. We need to know where
our own vision stops, where our limits and boundaries are.

Daily Prayer

*Help me to walk today in Your light so that I may truly
lead others on a God-centered path.*

May 17

I have a baptism to be baptized with and I'm under
pressure until it happens.
Luke 12:50

Life often calls us to face a particular crisis or challenge.
Trying to sidestep it only highlights its insistent call to our
deeper consciousness and conscience. It's only when we're broken apart that we can be put together at a higher level. It's in
the places where we're cracked that the light shines through.

Daily Prayer

**Give me the courage today to be baptized in the waters of
Your will.**

May 18

Heavenly Parent, forgive them, for they do not know what
they are doing.
Luke 23:34

Like Gandhi bowing to the divine in his assassin, Jesus forgives his executioners, It's important for us to know that
people need forgiveness, even those who crucify us and cause
us suffering, the very ones we want to consider "our enemies."

Daily Prayer

*Let me not turn anyone into an enemy today no matter how
hurt or neglected I may feel.*

May 19

No one can experience God's reign without being born
again from above.
John 3:3

The source of spiritual growth is both within and beyond us,
calling us again and again to enter the birth canal of transition
to new life and transformation. It takes a high quality of spiritual practice to enter that birth canal willingly.

Daily Prayer

*May I be willing to let go of the life I've planned in order to
receive the life God wants for me.*

May 20

I have come that you may have life and have it abundantly.
John 10:10

How sad that so many people see religion as something that
inhibits and restricts life. The institutions may do that,
because they tend to worship their own structures, but the
teachings on which those institutions are founded are life
enhancing.

Daily Prayer

*Thank You for filling me with Your life today in every part
of my being where I allow you to enter.*

May 21

I am resurrection and life; those who believe in me, even if
they die, will live.
John 11:25

Martin Buber reminds us that eternity is not an endless suc-
cession of moments but one eternal present. Eternal life is in
this present moment and is therefore unconcerned with death.
Being an "Easter person" provides a way of living in the here
and now.

Daily Prayer

*Let me trust Your power to raise whatever is dead in me for
You are a God of the living.*

May 22

If two make peace with one another in the same house, they
will say to the mountain, "Be moved!" and it will be moved.
Gospel of Thomas 48

We should never underestimate the depth of challenge
involved in achieving domestic peace; it is among those with
whom we live most closely that harmony often
seems most elusive.

Daily Prayer

*If I don't move mountains today, let me at least grow in
harmony with someone close to me.*

May 23

Blessed is the man who has labored; he has found life.
Gospel of Thomas 58

Suffering can lead to bitterness and despair but it can also lead to growth and life. I have often seen two people with an almost identical burden; and yet, one chooses life by picking up that cross while the other chooses death by shrinking from it.

Daily Prayer

I don't ask for suffering today, but if it comes, let it be a gateway to life, not a reason for complaint and despair.

May 24

Whoever drinks from my mouth will be as I am, and I shall
be that person, and the hidden things will be revealed
to that person.
Gospel of Thomas 108

The closeness of mystical union is described here as an identity between the human and the divine. The word "mystic"
comes from a root meaning "to be silent," for this kind of
experience goes beyond all human language and description.

Daily Prayer

Let all that I experience today draw me closer to You.

May 25

My prayer now is that a beginning may take place in you.
Secret Book of James 11:1

What a wonderful prayer. If only our every moment could be a new beginning. Paul Cezanne said that there is a moment of time passing by right now and we must become that moment.

Daily Prayer

Let this day be a beginning for me no matter how many endings my life has endured.

May 26

This is the right time. God's reign brushes against us. Open
your minds and accept this good news.
Mark 1:15

Jesus lived in an occupied nation where Caesar's reign was
everything; but he points us to God's reign where Caesar's rule
is inconsequential and he invites us to trust this inbreaking
divine reality that is always so close to us.

Daily Prayer

*Help me to understand that today is not "just another day"
but "the right time," a time when Your reign is at my door.*

May 27

Do we light a lamp and then extinguish it or do we put it on
a lampstand?
Mark 4:21

Our lights are meant to shine, not for our glory, but for God's.
We need therefore to let our lights shine. What would that
actually mean for each of us today?

Daily Prayer

**Let my light shine today, for it is a reflection of
Your light in our world.**

May 28

God's reign is like a tiny seed that grows into a large shrub
where birds make their nests in the shade.
Mark 4:31 & 32

No moment is too small to reflect God's glory and promote
God's reign. Wherever God reigns, others can find a place of
rest and refreshment.

Daily Prayer

*Let me not despise the small steps along my way because
they too belong to You.*

May 29

Who do you say that I am?
Mark 8:29

At some point we have to decide whether Jesus' words merit our response, whether or not we're willing to change our life. This has nothing to do with deciding to wear the label "Christian" or put a cross on a chain around our neck.

Daily Prayer

*I don't want simply to find these teachings interesting;
I want to be transformed by them.*

May 30

Salt is good but if it gets mixed with other things until it has
lost its saltiness, how can you regain its flavor?
Mark 9:49

We need to cherish and cultivate the deep truth that is in each
of us before it gets diluted by the demands and distractions of
our secular society. Or, on the other hand, we may need to find
what has already been diluted and replace it with something
that has the divine flavor.

Daily Prayer

***Let my life be savory and flavorful today, well seasoned with
Your love.***

May 31

Every tree is known by its fruits.
Gospel Q 21

Even our secular wisdom tells us that the proof of the pudding
is in the eating of it. Words are cheap, religious words more
perhaps than any others. Their truth is tested by their impact
on the real world where people's lives are affected.

Daily Prayer

***Send my roots rain today, and let my life be fruitful in
Your service.***

June 1

The poor widow who just put a few pennies in the collection
plate has given more than anyone else today.
Mark 12:43

God knows the supreme value of the gift of the heart, something not calculated by society's standards of philanthropy. A
generous and spontaneous gift is a wonderful work of love. No
wonder Jesus marvelled at this widow's simple greatness.

Daily Prayer

Let me give of myself today sincerely and generously.

June 2

Wherever in the world the good news is proclaimed, what this woman has done will be told in memory of her.
Mark 14:9

Jesus gives high praise to a generous woman who has anointed him with expensive ointment, despite the protests of some who profess concern about such an extravagant waste of money.

Daily Prayer

Let me realize those times that call for more than frugality.

June 3

It is a blessing to hunger and thirst for a God-centered life;
you will be filled.
Matthew 5:6

We have an appetite for many things but are we really hungry
and thirsty to know God and to embrace God's will for us?
Thomas Aquinas said that all it takes to be a great saint is
really to want it.

Daily Prayer

*May I want a God-centered life as much as I want food
when I'm hungry or drink when I'm thirsty.*

June 4

Not everyone who cries out "Lord, Lord!" will enter
God's reign but only the person who does the will of my
Heavenly Parent.
Gospel Q 22

Measure the religiosity of a place of prayer and of the people
who attend services there, not by the prayers and rituals
within its sacred space, but by what happens in the parking
lot and on the street after the service is over.

Daily Prayer

*May my deeds run fast enough to keep pace with
my words today.*

June 5

If someone forces you to go one mile, go a second mile as well.
Matthew 5:41

In the occupied Palestine of Jesus' time, any Jew could be con-
scripted by a Roman soldier to carry his gear for a mile. To go
a second mile would mean moving from slave-like obligation
to the free gift of a person who is equal.

Daily Prayer

*Help me to realize that real life doesn't begin to happen
until I go more than half way.*

June 6

Be children of your Heavenly Parent whose sun rises on bad
and good alike and whose rain falls both on the God-centered
and the wayward.
Matthew 5:45

We are invited to meet all our fellow human beings with
unconditional acceptance and good will. It is a challenge to be
as non-judgmental as the sun and rain.

Daily Prayer

*Help me to realize that I haven't reached sanctity just
because I'm nice to my friends.*

June 7

If you forgive others their failings, then your Heavenly Parent
will also forgive you; but if you don't forgive others, neither
will your failings be forgiven.
Matthew 6:14 & 15

If we don't open to others a door to the future extending
beyond their past mistakes, how can we ask God to open such
a door for us? And isn't that what we most want others to
offer us?

Daily Prayer

*May I always offer others a future that is greater than the
mistakes of their past.*

June 8

Don't worry about tomorrow; it will bring worries of its own.
Today's troubles are enough for today.
Matthew 6:34

The great wisdom traditions all focus on the present moment,
the here and now, as the only real place for our practice.
Neither yesterday nor tomorrow are real.

Daily Prayer

*Don't let me get so hooked on tomorrow that I neglect the
task and the challenge that face me today.*

June 9

Whatever town or village you enter, find out who in it
deserves your ministry and stay there until you leave.
Gospel Q 30

This teaching portrays a lifestyle totally dependent on the
generosity and hospitality of people who understand themselves as brothers and sisters, dwelling together on an earth
that is truly the Lord's.

Daily Prayer

*Help me to be able both to give and receive hospitality in
my encounters with others today.*

June 10

If you who are far from perfect know how to give gifts to your
children, how much more will your Heavenly Parent give
good things to those who ask.
Gospel Q 36

Good human parenting provides but a pale example of God's
love. God is for us, not against us, wanting our own good and
growth more than we can ever imagine.

Daily Prayer

*I can never be adequately grateful to God for loving me so
constantly, so completely, so compellingly.*

June 11

If anyone will not welcome you or listen to your words, shake off the dust from your feet and leave that house or town.
Matthew 10:14

People receive a teaching when they're ready for it. If the readiness is not there, it's just as well to move on to find a soil that's more receptive. Spiritual teaching at its best is always an invitation, not a forced ultimatum.

Daily Prayer

Help me to be present to others, not with the words I need to say, but with the words they need to hear.

June 12

Are not two sparrows sold for a penny? Yet not one of them
falls to the ground without your Heavenly Parent knowing
about it. So don't be afraid; you are of more value than
a flock of sparrows.
Gospel Q 46

Our instinctual fear is that no one really loves us or cares
about us. And yet the truth is that we are loved and cared for
beyond our wildest imaginings.

Daily Prayer

*I thank God for loving me so much that I was called into
being as one of a kind, the one and only me that God
wanted in the universe.*

June 13

My yoke is easy and my burden light.
Matthew 11:30

The word "yoke" refers to a farm implement to which two animals are attached for work. Any path of discipleship is rightly called a yoke because it is worn by two. Jews are yoked to the Torah, just as Christians are yoked to Jesus. Hindus use the same root word in speaking of the various yogas by which they are yoked to the divine.

Daily Prayer

Help me to know that my yoke is light because You are always my yoke-partner.

June 14

It is out of the abundance of the heart that the mouth speaks.
Matthew 12:34b

We need to pay attention to our words; over time they reveal
our basic values, the places where we've pinned our hearts.

Daily Prayer

*Help me to be attentive to my words today, since they teach
me the values I most deeply cherish.*

June 15

A farmer went out to sow. Some seed fell along the path; some
on rocky ground; some among thorns; and some on cultivated
ground where it could grow.
Matthew 13:4-8

The seed is always adequate; only the soil is sometimes
lacking. Attentiveness, readiness, and receptivity are
everything when it comes to spiritual growth.

Daily Prayer

*Let my soil be ready today for all the good and healthy seeds
God wants to plant in me.*

June 16

Wherever two or three of you are gathered together in my
name, I will be there among you.
Matthew 18:20

When we meet each other in terms of the divine reality that
binds us, then God joins such a holy community in an especially powerful and empowering way.

Daily Prayer

*Help me to find friends with whom I can share not only pol-
itics and sports, but the deeper issues of my life with You.*

June 17

Whoever is near me is near fire, but whoever is far from
me is far from the kingdom.
Gospel of Thomas 82

Jesus' presence has all the ambiguity of fire. It warms and
burns; it illuminates and destroys; it excites and frightens.

Daily Prayer

*Although I'm afraid as well as attracted, I do want to be
with You.*

June 18

Martha, you are worried and concerned about many things but
one thing only is necessary. Mary has chosen the better part
and it won't be taken away from her.
Luke 10:41

Martha is busy in the kitchen, while Mary sits at Jesus'
feet and learns wisdom. In this statement Jesus responds
to Martha's complaints by challenging the accepted role of
women. He affirms the freedom of women to come out of the
kitchen both to learn and to teach spiritual wisdom.

Daily Prayer

*Let me get beyond the sexism of society and recognize in
every woman (including myself, if I am a woman) Your
image and the full dignity of Your creation.*

June 19

Buyers and merchants will not enter the places of my father.
Gospel of Thomas 64

It's not the profession but the mentality that is the issue here.
The greed is the problem and it's not so much in our work as
in our attachment to it. For it's what's in our hearts not what's
on our business cards that finally matters to God.

Daily Prayer

*While I'm busy making a living may I remember to
make a life too.*

June 20

Everyone who hears my teachings and acts on them will be like a wise person who builds a house on a solid foundation.
Matthew 7:24

What does it really mean to build the house of our lives on the teachings of Jesus? The bedrock foundation consists of wisdom, compassion, justice, love, and peace.

Daily Prayer

Let all my words and actions today be built on the foundation of Your love.

June 21

You are not to be called teacher for you have one teacher and
you are all students.
Matthew 23:8

The fellowship to which Jesus calls people is always one of
brothers and sisters, never one involving a corporate ladder or
hierarchy of any kind.

Daily Prayer

*May God be my teacher today and may I have the open ears
of a student.*

June 22

The queen of the South will rise at the judgment with this
generation and condemn them, for she came from far away
to hear the wisdom of Solomon and someone greater than
Solomon is here.
Gospel Q 41

The Hebrew Bible speaks of the queen of Sheba (modern
Ethiopia) coming all the way from Africa to learn wisdom
from King Solomon. And yet Jesus' contemporaries often fail
to appreciate the wisdom that is so close at hand in him.

Daily Prayer

*Help me to realize that I don't have to go a great distance to
hear Your wisdom.*

June 23

You will not be able to observe the coming of God's reign nor
say that it is here or there, for it is right in front of
you all the time.
Gospel Q 79

It's so much easier to play with calendars of future divine
intervention rather than recognize the blessings we receive
today, responding to them with open hearts.

Daily Prayer

*Help me not to miss what is right in front of me today,
because that's where I'll find You and Your will for me.*

June 24

What I'm teaching doesn't originate with me but with the
one who sent me.
John 7:16

Jesus should not be the object of our final attention; he is the
vehicle bringing us to the divine reality, the divine truth, and
the divine love.

Daily Prayer

*Help me to live by Your truth, wherever and however
I learn it.*

June 25

Those who trust in God will perform the works I performed
and will be able to do even greater deeds.
John 14:12

People who see Jesus primarily as someone to be worshipped
find it confusing to be challenged to excel Jesus himself
in performing great feats of faith. Not many sermons are
preached on this text!

Daily Prayer

*Help me to realize that there are no limits to what I can do
when I am acting in Your Spirit.*

June 26

I am the good shepherd, the kind of shepherd who gives his life for his sheep.
John 9:11

True compassion is more than empty words and futile gestures. It demands committed love, something strong enough to die for. The true shepherd is easy to distinguish from the hireling who is in it only for the money.

Daily Prayer

Help me to be a good shepherd, providing real leadership and compassion in all the circumstances of my day.

June 27

Follow me and I'll make you fishers of people.
Mark 1:17

Pulling people up from the water means calling them to a
change of consciousness, to rebirth. Those who follow a path
of greater consciousness can help others to be fished out of the
waters of conventional wisdom.

Daily Prayer

*Help me to be a fisher of people today by calling them to a
consciousness of You.*

June 28

There is a light within a man of light and it illuminates the
whole world. When it does not shine, there is darkness.
Gospel of Thomas 24

The image of God, the spark of the divine that is within each
of us, is a light that can shine forth as far as we permit it.
When this light does not shine, we add to the darkness of war,
hate, prejudice, greed, and pride.

Daily Prayer

*You are my strength. You are my light. You are my life. You
are my healing.*

June 29

I shall give you what no eye has seen, what no ear has heard
and no hand has touched, and what has not come into the
human heart.
Gospel of Thomas 17

The divine mystery is beyond all the data of the sensible
world that we can measure and quantify and beyond all the
cogitations of the rational mind as well.

Daily Prayer

*Let me be ready to receive all the divine life that
You offer me today.*

June 30

If those who lead you say, "Look, the kingdom is in heaven," then the birds of heaven will precede you. If they say, "It is in the sea," then the fish will precede you. Rather, the kingdom is within you and outside you.

Gospel of Thomas 3

A clear statement that God's reign is not hiding in a secret place or waiting for a secret time; it wants only our readiness, attentiveness, and receptivity.

Daily Prayer

Let me discern Your reign in all that is inside and outside of me.

July 1

One does not live by bread alone.
Gospel Q 6

After fasting forty days and nights in the wilderness, Jesus
is portrayed as quoting this verse of Deuteronomy to Satan.
How extraordinary it is, when suffering the pangs of a
terrible hunger, to remember that we are more than
what we eat and drink.

Daily Prayer

*Let me not get so caught up in my bodily needs today that I
forget my need for Your words, Your power, and Your truth.*

July 2

Worship the Lord your God, serving God alone.
Gospel Q 8

Again Jesus responds to Satan with a verse from Deuteronomy.
It's always the first commandment that is the most difficult.
Devout Muslims remind themselves each day that only God is
God. And the Hindus teach us that God is one, though called
by many names.

Daily Prayer

***Don't let me put anything or anyone ahead of
Your will today.***

July 3

Do not put the Lord your God to the test.
Gospel Q 7

Jesus directs a third verse from Deuteronomy to humankind's great tempter. Jesus does not expect that angels will save him from the circumstances of a human life. Jesus asks for no special privileges. He is here to serve, to love, and to give of himself completely.

Daily Prayer

Let me live this day in gratitude to You, not in a spirit of complaint.

July 4

The Spirit of the Lord is upon me, because God has anointed
me to bring good news to the poor.
Luke 4:18a

Jesus is portrayed as reading these words from Isaiah in his
hometown synagogue. Jesus realizes that day that these words
are fulfilled in his own life and ministry. He is God's anointed
servant, one with good news for God's poor.

Daily Prayer

*Let me live this day anointed by Your word as one who
brings good news to all those in need.*

July 5

God has sent me to proclaim release to the captives and
recovery of sight to the blind.
Luke 4:18b

Continuing to read from the Isaiah scroll in his hometown
synagogue, Jesus has insight into his own vocation to bring
freedom to those who are tied up by fear, despair, or sin and to
open all eyes to God's light.

Daily Prayer

*May the scales of my blindness fall so that my eyes see in
Your light.*

July 6

God has sent me to let the oppressed go free, to proclaim the
year of the Lord's favor.
Luke 4:19

The text of Isaiah talks about a special Jubilee when the sabbath year is multiplied by the sabbath, i.e., the fiftieth year,
since seven times seven is forty-nine. But from Jesus' perspective, that once-in-fifty-years moment is in every here and now.

Daily Prayer

**Help me to realize that there is no holier moment
than this one.**

July 7

It's a fact that prophets aren't welcome in their hometowns.
Luke 4:24

Our natural tendency is to think that the ordinary is unimportant; and yet, when we begin to see things better, we realize that nothing is ordinary because everything manifests the mystery of the divine. We are surrounded by miracle, even in our hometown, even in the people we see everyday.

Daily Prayer

**Help me not to confuse what's unusual with what's
important today.**

July 8

Be silent and come out of him.
Luke 4:35

Jesus' words to a possessed man remind us that it is the noisy chatter of an undisciplined mind that can most damage us. If we stop listening to the voices of negativity, they have no choice but to leave us alone.

Daily Prayer

Let me give my ears to God's words today, not to society's noise.

July 9

I must proclaim the good news of God's reign to the other cities also; for I was sent for this purpose.
Luke 4:43

Jesus doesn't wander aimlessly. He has a sense of mission and
purpose. He wants people to know that God's reign is available to them in each passing moment of their lives.

Daily Prayer

*Let all those I meet today have a better sense of Your avail-
ability to them because of me and what I say and do.*

July 10

Put out into the deep water and let down your
nets for a catch.
Luke 5:4

The biggest fish swim in the deepest parts of the sea; the most
important elements of our lives lie deepest in our unconscious.
We need to let our nets down to bring these parts of ourselves
to greater consciousness.

Daily Prayer

May I not fear the deep waters today.

July 11

Do not be afraid; from now on you will be catching people.
Luke 5:10

It's an extraordinary responsibility to exert an influence on others. It happens by our example, whether we want it to or not. What's important is that our influence always be towards greater life and greater freedom.

Daily Prayer

Let me draw people to You today, not to my own ego with its all too full agenda.

July 12

Of course I want you to be clean.
Luke 5:13

Jesus responds to the leper with a strong statement of his desire to heal him. There's never a lack on Jesus' part of the will to heal. The sick person's will to trust is what is most often lacking in these situations.

Daily Prayer

Let me live this day with the confidence that You love me more than I love myself, that You want to help me more even than I want to be helped.

July 13

Go and show yourself to a priest, as Moses commanded; make
an offering for your cleansing, for a testimony to them.
Luke 5:14

Even though Jesus deals with people apart from the Temple,
he affirms both its personnel and its practices. Religion has a
valid role to play, as long as it remembers that it is the vehicle
and not the value.

Daily Prayer

**Let me not worship my religion today but the One to
whom it points.**

July 14

Friend, your sins are forgiven you.
Luke 5:20

What wonderful news, to be offered a future that is bigger than all the limitations of our past. That's what Jesus reminded people of day in and day out. That's what he continues to remind us of today.

Daily Prayer

Thank You for the future You open up for me in this moment.

July 15

What is easier, to forgive your sins or to tell you to
stand up and walk?
Luke 5:23

Bondage is bondage, whatever form it takes. And healing
means freedom, wherever it touches our human condition.
Jesus brought freedom from bondage and healing
to all he met.

Daily Prayer

Help me to hear Your word and to stand up and walk today.

July 16

Get up, pick up your bed, and go to your home.
Luke 5:24

There are areas of life where we are immobile and lifeless. We need to be open to healing there and take these parts of ourselves home, i.e., owning them, even as we turn them over to God's healing power.

Daily Prayer

Let me acknowledge the part of me that is lifeless and pick that part up, taking it home to fuller life and movement in You.

July 17

Follow me.
Luke 5:27

Such a simple phrase and yet how often Jesus turned a life around by speaking it. St. Paul reminds us that others should follow our example as we follow Jesus' example. And in following Jesus, we are pursuing God's ways in the world.

Daily Prayer

Let me follow You today and let me help others to follow You too.

July 18

Have you not read what David did when he and his
companions were hungry?
Luke 6:3

When David and his companions were hungry, they entered
the sanctuary and ate the bread dedicated to God. David did
what was forbidden when human need was greater than the
law. Jesus too sees laws as provisional guidelines, not
absolutes. The absolutes are love of God, love of oneself,
and love of our neighbor.

Daily Prayer

*Help me to remember the difference between the guideline
and the goal.*

July 19

I ask you, is it lawful to do good or to do harm on the
Sabbath, to save life or to destroy it?
Luke 6:9

Again and again Jesus calls our attention to the priority of
human need over the guidelines of conventional religion.
God's happy to have you miss the Sunday morning service in
order to stop and help the motorist in need...even if you solo
in the choir.

Daily Prayer

*Don't let my religious practice keep me away from
You today.*

July 20

Stretch out your hand.
Luke 6:10

First Jesus had asked this man with a withered hand to come and stand by him; now he asks him to stretch out that deformed hand. Jesus encounters people one on one and often asks them, as in this case, to do something as a sign of their trust in God.

Daily Prayer

Help me to hold out to You all that is sick and deformed in my life and to trust Your desire and Your power to heal me.

July 21

Damn you rich people; you already have your consolation.
Luke 6:24

Many people seem so over-rewarded for what they do—like some CEOs or professional athletes. Others labor long and hard with so little recompense. Jesus' heart goes out to the latter, as should ours.

Daily Prayer

Let me be poured out in Your service today, not counting on any material reward to match my efforts.

July 22

Damn you, gorged with food; one day you'll be hungry.
Luke 6:25a

How often those of us who have never lacked food complain at the first feeling of hunger and say: "I'm starving." How obscene such a remark is in a world where so many people really are starving.

Daily Prayer

Help me to keep my life in perspective today, realizing how much I have in comparison with those who are truly needy.

July 23

Damn you, mocking others now; one day you'll be
feeling bad.
Luke 6:25b

There's no easier way to get a laugh than by putting someone
else down—in our family, at our workplace, in social gather-
ings. How little sensitivity this shows on our part for the
feelings of others. How little love this shows for
their infinite worth.

Daily Prayer

*Help me today to feel things from the other side, i.e., from
the perspective of those I meet along my way.*

July 24

Damn you, when others fawn over you; that's what always
happened to the false prophets.
Luke 6:26

It shouldn't be our goal just to gain the adulation of others.
Our concern should be to take some steps forward for what is
true, for what is just, for what is right in God's eyes.

Daily Prayer

*Don't let me act today for the approval of others but to do
what is right in Your sight.*

July 25

If you love those who love you, so what? Even corrupt
politicians do that.
Gospel Q 16a

We really should take no credit for being nice to the people
who are nice to us. The test of virtue is with those who don't
naturally appeal to us, who don't make an effort to please us,
who don't easily fit our agenda.

Daily Prayer

*Help me to be alert today to the way I deal with those people
I don't find particularly attractive or interesting.*

July 26

Love your enemies, do good, and lend, expecting
nothing in return.
Gospel Q 16b

We live in a society where we claim that there is "no free
lunch." Everything can be bought and everyone has his or her
price. And yet, Jesus calls us to act in an entirely unconventional way, a way that seems absurd in our
"bottom line" society.

Daily Prayer

Let me try today to give to others with no strings attached.

July 27

Why do you pay me lip service as a teacher but not do
what I say?
Egerton Gospel 3:5

How often Jesus points up the disparity between our words
and our deeds. We have to guard our lips so that they don't
outrun our commitments.

Daily Prayer

**Help me to hear Your teachings today by translating
them into actions.**

July 28

It is out of the abundance of the heart that the mouth speaks.
Gospel Q 21

In a world where talk is cheap this is a sobering reflection. If we could replay some of our office chatter, some of our dinner table conversation, would we be embarrassed to realize that this says something about where our central values are?

Daily Prayer

Help me today to focus on what is really important to me before I start talking without thinking.

July 29

Why do you call me "Lord, Lord!" and not do what I tell you?
Gospel Q 22

Jesus tells us again and again that "God talk" is cheap. It has no more value than the campaign promises of corrupt politicians or the religious rhetoric of televangelists. God is where people are being helped, where peace is built through the pursuit of justice, where compassion is shown to people on the margins of society.

Daily Prayer

May my deeds far outstrip my words today.

July 30

Not even in Israel have I found such faith.
Gospel Q 23

An officer in the Roman army of occupation approaches
Jesus, requesting a cure. He sees no need for Jesus to come
to his house, recognizing his ability to bring healing even at
a distance. Jesus marvels at this level of trust from a Gentile
and a pagan.

Daily Prayer

*I am not worthy that You should come under my roof; just
say the word and I will be healed.*

July 31

Do not weep.
Luke 7:13

A widow is accompanying the dead body of her only son to the burial site when Jesus stops the little procession with these words. He restores the son to his mother, reminding us that in life all endings are only transitions.

Daily Prayer

Help me to place in Your hands everything that ends and dies for me today.

August 1

Young man, get up.
Luke 7:14

It's a dramatic moment as Jesus addresses these words to the dead man, the only son of a widowed mother. We're told that Jesus "gave him to his mother"—an important detail in a world where women belonged to a man's home and were dependent on men for their subsistence. Where so many others ignored women, Jesus acknowledged them.

Daily Prayer

If any part of me is dead this day, may God restore it to life.

August 2

It's a blessing if you don't get offended by what I'm doing.
Luke 7:23

Jesus' whole life and ministry clash with conventional wisdom
and expectations. It's no wonder that many people would and
indeed did take offense at such a disturbing and
disruptive presence.

Daily Prayer

*I pray that I will not take offense when Your word contra-
dicts my ego needs and the conventions of my society.*

August 3

What did you go out into the wilderness to see, a reed shaken
by the wind?
Luke 7:24

The wilderness is the place of contrasts: night and day, cold
and heat, God and Satan. John the Baptist lives in this wilderness, a place where no one weak or wavering could
ever survive.

Daily Prayer

*Let me not be a reed shaken by every wind but a reed in
which Your Spirit blows.*

August 4

What did you go out into the wilderness to see, someone
dressed in a ten thousand dollar suit?
Gospel Q 24a

The wilderness is a place for the cosmic conflict between good
and evil, not for an empty display of the world's vanities.
John the Baptist is a crucial figure in history, not a mere
storewindow mannequin.

Daily Prayer

*Help me, like John the Baptist, to have a bold voice to
proclaim You.*

August 5

Those who wear expensive clothes and bathe in luxury live in
the wealthy suburbs.
Gospel Q 24b

We see here once again the contrast between the conventional
wisdom regarding true success (two cars and the house in the
suburbs) and the subversive wisdom embodied in the life and
ministry of both John the Baptist and Jesus himself.

Daily Prayer

*Help me to choose what is truly valuable in life and not
what is simply superficially appealing.*

August 6

Did you go out to see a prophet, and even more
than a prophet?
Gospel Q 24c

A prophet is one who speaks for God, who articulates God's word, God's message, at a particular juncture of human history. Jesus declares John to be not only a prophet but more than a prophet, since John has such a special relationship to the beginning of Jesus' own ministry and public life.

Daily Prayer

Help me to speak Your word today and to be Your prophet.

August 7

Among those born of women, none is greater than John; but
the least in God's reign is ahead of John.
Gospel Q 24d

Although he is the greatest apocalyptic preacher of his time,
John does not share the consciousness of Jesus' new understanding of God's reign. Jesus doesn't see God's coming as a
vengeful judgment but as an ever-present loving availability.

Daily Prayer

*Help me to believe and proclaim Your ever-present reign by
my every thought, word, and deed today.*

August 8

Some of you are never happy, saying that John the Baptist has a demon, while I'm a drunkard.
Gospel Q 26a

We can find all kinds of excuses for closing ourselves to God's word. We can twist and turn to avoid God's challenges to us. We can even blame the messenger when the message is too disturbing to our conventional wisdom.

Daily Prayer

Don't let me avoid Your word today and Your challenge to me by fabricating excuses and blaming circumstances.

August 9

Wisdom is proved right by all her children.
Gospel Q 26b

Jesus is a teacher of wisdom, an unconventional wisdom, a
radical wisdom, even a subversive wisdom. This wisdom is
proved, not by rational arguments, but by
the lives of those who embody it.

Daily Prayer

May divine wisdom be made flesh in my life today.

August 10

This woman's sins, though many, have been forgiven, because she has shown great love. But the one to whom little is forgiven, loves little.
Luke 7:47

This is not, of course, an excuse to sin so as to grow in love, but a recognition that the awareness of how much even the best of us has been forgiven opens up a tremendous space for a corresponding love.

Daily Prayer

Help me to love You today like this woman, aware of how much Your forgiveness embraces my life.

August 11

Your faith has healed you; go in peace.
Luke 7:50

Jesus is not a magician. We are called to trust God and to trust Jesus' role in mediating God's power and presence in the world. It is this trust that brings healing, wholeness, and peace.

Daily Prayer

Help me to trust You today and to experience Your healing and Your peace.

August 12

Where is your faith?
Luke 8:25

There is a storm at sea and Jesus is sleeping in the boat. How often this replicates the circumstances of our lives—we are in dire straits and God seems absent. And yet those moments are precisely the situations where we're called on to trust God and to know that God's love and care never sleep.

Daily Prayer

Let me trust You, even in those moments when You seem absent or sleeping.

August 13

What is your name?
Luke 8:30

When Jesus asks this question of the evil spirits possessing the Gerasene demoniac, they replay that their name is "Legion." This has special significance in a country occupied by the foreign legions of Rome. But whether one or many, they leave the man at Jesus' command.

Daily Prayer

Cast out every evil spirit in me and fill me with Your spirit today.

August 14

Return to your home and declare how much God has
done for you.
Luke 8:39

The cured Gerasene demoniac is sent as a witness to the fact
that the God of Israel is still alive and powerful to heal and
make whole. The man who is cured becomes a missionary to
his own family and friends and we notice that he is sent not to
proclaim what Jesus has done but what God has done
through Jesus.

Daily Prayer

*Let me share with my family and friends today some of the
many wonders You work in my life.*

August 15

Someone has touched me for I notice that power has
gone out from me.
Luke 8:46

The hemorrhaging woman who touched Jesus' tzizit (the
tassels of his talit or prayer shawl) has been healed by God's
power moving through Jesus as its conduit. Jesus seems
almost like a battery charged with God's power.

Daily Prayer

*Let Your power flow into me today, charging me with
Your energy.*

August 16

Do not fear. Only believe and she will be healed.
Luke 8:50

Jairus is the leader of the local synagogue and he came to Jesus
for help because his twelve-year-old daughter was sick. Now
word has come that she is dead and all seems lost but Jesus
encourages him to stand fast in his faith and proceeds to heal
the girl.

Daily Prayer

***Let me realize that no situation is final for God,
not even death.***

August 17

You give them something to eat.
Luke 9:13

Surrounded by hungry crowds, Jesus challenges his disciples to feed them. Jesus doesn't act without the cooperation of everyone there, for he is teaching his followers how to act, even in his absence, with compassion and love.

Daily Prayer

Help me to act in this world today in cooperation with You, not expecting You to act in my place.

August 18

Let these words sink into your ears; I am going to be betrayed
into human hands.
Luke 9:44

We want good things for those we love, good things as we
understand them. Jesus' disciples want him to have victory
and success, not torture and death. And yet, God's will sometimes leads us to the dark valley of death.

Daily Prayer

*I don't ask to be spared from the consequences of human
life today but to be strengthened to embrace the divine will,
even in difficult times.*

August 19

No one who puts a hand to the plow and looks back is ready
for God's reign.
Luke 9:62

We don't get anywhere being double-minded, trying to serve
two masters, trying to go in two opposite directions at the
same time. We need to be attentive, present, wholly in the
moment with its task and challenge.

Daily Prayer

*Help me to be single-minded today, attentive to what is at
hand in every moment.*

August 20

Whoever listens to you listens to me and whoever rejects
you rejects me, and whoever rejects me rejects the one
who sent me.
Gospel Q 31

Jesus' teaching and ministry do not derive from his ego but
from the will of his Heavenly Parent. To oppose his work of
healing, forgiveness, and compassion is not to oppose Jesus
but to oppose the God working through him.

Daily Prayer

*Let me be aligned with Your will today, so that it is not so
much me acting as You acting in me.*

August 21

I watched Satan fall from heaven like a flash of lightning.
Luke 10:18

The power of God's reign is so manifest in Jesus' words and
deeds that Satan's reign is self-destructing. Evil has no real
power wherever the teachings of Jesus are heard and obeyed.

Daily Prayer

*Let me not fear evil but let me fear to live apart from Your
word and Your will.*

August 22

I have given you authority to tread on snakes and scorpions,
and over all the power of the enemy; and nothing
will hurt you.
Luke 10:19

Some literal interpreters of the Bible handle snakes in
churches and sadly are often killed. In the Jewish idiom of the
time, "snakes and scorpions" referred to dangerous and hereti-
cal teachings. Error has no power over one who is imbued
with God's truth.

Daily Prayer

*Let me fear nothing today, except being separated from
Your presence and Your truth.*

August 23

Don't rejoice that the spirits submit to you but rejoice that
your names are written in heaven.
Luke 10:20

The Jewish New Year (Rosh Hashanah) greeting is to wish
that others be inscribed in the book of life. This is an ancient
metaphor for being aligned with God's will, for being in
God's favor or good graces.

Daily Prayer

*Don't let me ego trip on what I'm able to achieve today but
let me rather be happy that You choose to use me in doing
Your work.*

August 24

If the one who showed compassion is the true neighbor, then
you should go and do likewise.
Luke 10:37

The Parable of the Good Samaritan is one of Jesus' greatest
stories. Official clergy hasten past the person in need to fulfill
their religious duties in the Temple, but a despised Samaritan
stops to show the compassion that is the true sign of God's
presence in the world.

Daily Prayer

*Help me to be like the Good Samaritan; help me to be a real
neighbor to those who need me today.*

August 25

Every kingdom divided against itself becomes a desert, and
house falls on house.
Gospel Q 37

Some of Jesus' opponents alleged that his works were from
Satan. But how could Jesus be allied with Satan when Satan is
being expelled wherever Jesus is present? If Satan's kingdom
is that absurd, then its ruin is indeed assured.

Daily Prayer

Let me be undivided today in attending to Your will.

August 26

Blessed are those who hear the word of God and obey it.
Gospel Q 40

The message is repeated so many times. No other criteria serve
more to identify the true disciples of Jesus than hearing God's
word and obeying it. Jesus' teachings are eminently practical;
the tree is always known by its fruit.

Daily Prayer

*Let me seek the greatest blessing today, the ability to discern
Your will and do it.*

August 27

Give for alms those things that are within; and see, everything
will be clean for you.
Luke 11:41

We often see Jesus as a teacher of kavanah, the Hebrew term
for inwardness and intentionality. The external deed is only
half real if it is divorced from the intentions of the heart, just
as the intentions of the heart are only half real if they don't
translate into real actions in the world. As usual, the truth is
found in the balance.

Daily Prayer

***Let the deeds of my hands and the intentions of
my heart be one today.***

August 28

Do not be afraid; you are of more value than many sparrows.
Gospel Q 46

It's so natural to think that we have to merit God's love or that God would love us more if we were more like Mother Teresa or the Dalai Lama. But God loves us just as we are and God loves us for who we are and God loves us more than we can even imagine.

Daily Prayer

Help me not to doubt Your love for me, a love too over-whelming for me ever to understand.

August 29

Whoever speaks against me can be forgiven but whoever
curses the Holy Spirit cannot be forgiven.
Gospel Q 48

The Holy Spirit is God's active presence in the world. To curse
the Spirit, i.e., to place ourselves against that divine presence,
puts us in a place where we can't receive forgiveness, since
we're denying the very God who forgives.

Daily Prayer

*Let me help, not hinder, the action of Your spirit in the
world today.*

August 30

Take care! Be on your guard against all kinds of greed; for one's life does not consist in the abundance of possessions.
Luke 12:15

Making a life is not the same as making a living. Filling our lives with the consumer goods of our society doesn't necessarily fill our hearts. Without the divine reality, our lives and our hearts will always be empty.

Daily Prayer

Help me to use the goods of this world, while not giving my heart to them.

August 31

Sell your possessions and give alms. Make purses for yourselves that don't wear out, an unfailing treasure in heaven where no thief comes near and no moth destroys.
Gospel Q 54

Again we are told that there is no problem in owning possessions but there is a problem in clinging to them, in being attached to them. That's why the Buddha taught that we must see all things as being on fire, too hot to cling to for long.

Daily Prayer

Help me not to confuse the goods of this world with the true good of being aligned with You and Your will.

September 1

Be dressed for action and have your lamps lit.
Luke 12:35

We must always be attentive to the moment with its potential for revealing God and God's will. The "sacrament of the present moment" is one we must be ready to receive at all times. It is our lifeline to God.

Daily Prayer

Help me to become the moment that is passing by so that I may find You there.

September 2

You must be ready because I'm coming at an unexpected hour.
Gospel Q 55

Hundreds of years ago, the rabbis said that we must repent
the day before we die. And, of course, since we never know
when that day of death will be, we have no alternative but to
repent today. The hour is always unexpected unless
it is always expected.

Daily Prayer

*Help me to live every moment with the expectancy of
encountering You.*

September 3

If you untie your animals to give them food and drink on the Sabbath, shouldn't I also untie this woman from her eighteen-year illness on the Sabbath?
Luke 13:15

Time and again Jesus emphasizes that ritual laws are subordinate to the great commandment of love. Compassion, for Jesus, takes precedence over any of the demands of religious observance.

Daily Prayer

Let me make love the law of my life, a law to which all other laws are secondary.

September 4

When you plan a dinner party, invite the poor, the crippled, the lame, and the blind. It will be a blessing for you because they can't repay you.
Luke 14:14

This saying is well seasoned with the salt of unconventional wisdom. It runs contrary to how most of us would like to plan a party. Jesus challenges us to step outside of the conventional and the expected, to be ready for the God of surprises.

Daily Prayer

Help me to extend myself today beyond the bounds of social convention so that I might encounter some of the surprises You have in store for me.

September 5

Whoever comes to me and does not hate father and mother,
wife and children, brothers and sisters, yes, and even life itself,
cannot be my disciple.
Gospel Q 69

"Hate" is a strong word and we're told that this is typical of
Mideastern rhetoric. It's more, however, than mere rhetoric,
because there really is room for only one absolute value and
that niche cannot be a shared one.

Daily Prayer

*Help me to put You and Your will above everything and
everyone else today.*

September 6

If you're planning on building a tower, don't you first sit down and make a cost estimate to see if you have the funds to complete it?
Luke 14:28

How naturally Jesus moves our thinking from the common-sense of everyday life to the divine sense of walking a spiritual path. Do we have the resources to complete the task we've begun? Prayer and meditation, deeds of loving kindness, the support of the community, the study of spiritual texts—these are but a few of our resources.

Daily Prayer

Help me take stock of my life and make sure that I have the resources I need to walk in Your path.

September 7

Whoever is faithful in small matters is faithful also in greater ones; and whoever is dishonest in small matters is dishonest also in greater ones.

Luke 16:10

This is the spiritual law of exponential growth. The God-centered choice opens up more doors to a God-centered life; the ego-centered choice opens up more doors to an ego-centered life. Little steps often have big consequences.

Daily Prayer

Help me to be faithful in some of the little matters today that open me up to larger decisions for You and Your will.

September 8

The law and the prophets were in effect until John came; since then the good news of God's reign is proclaimed and all who want to are pressing their way into it.
Gospel Q 25

Although Jesus proclaims non-violence, more than once we see his sayings include force. He opens the door of God's reign so boldly that we are encouraged to press forward with all the energy we can muster.

Daily Prayer

Help me to put energy today in opening my life to Your reign.

September 9

It's impossible that people's consciences never be hurt but
damn those who are the cause of it.
Luke 17:1

If we're not ready to help others be open to God's reign, let's
at least not close the door in their face or put them off from
it by our example. Hindering others in their spiritual path is
certainly a sin we don't want on our conscience.

Daily Prayer

*Let nothing I do today hinder anyone else from being
open to You.*

September 10

If the same person offends you seven times a day and expresses
sorrow seven times, you should be forgiving.
Luke 17:4

Seven is a number of fullness here. It's not simply the number
before eight but the umber that means without number. We
want God to forgive us over and over again, and that means
that we need to exhibit that same behavior to others.

Daily Prayer

Help me to be a truly forgiving person today.

September 11

If you had faith the size of a mustard seed you could ask
this mulberry tree to grow in the lake instead and
it would obey you.
Gospel Q 78

These wild Mideastern images call our attention to the crucial significance of trusting God. Faith has accomplished even
greater things than transplanting trees into lake water.

Daily Prayer

*My sense of trust may seem small today but God can help
this small seed grow into a profound faith.*

September 12

When you've done all that you're supposed to do, you should still be aware that you're a worthless servant and have only done your duty.
Luke 17:10

Jesus is at great pains to point out that we can't get the upper hand on God by any of our good works. There is simply no room for complacency when we're talking about the work of God's reign. God's servants never retire nor do they earn bonuses.

Daily Prayer

Let me be content to try to do Your will in every way possible today, with no expectation of special kudos for services rendered.

September 13

It's great that this foreigner came back to thank me, but
weren't ten lepers made clean?
Luke 17:17

Ten lepers are cleansed but only the foreigner returns to
say thanks. How often we are counted among the other
nine, happy to receive God's blessings but too busy to be
properly grateful.

Daily Prayer

Let me not take God's gifts for granted today.

September 14

Will God not grant justice to the people who cry to
God day and night?
Luke 18:7

So often we engage in "prayer lite"—a passing wish or peti-
tion. But to be passionate for God's justice is to cry to God
about it day and night, to pray without ceasing, to pray from
the depths of our hearts.

Daily Prayer

*Let my prayer to You today be sincere, persistent, and from
my deepest heart.*

September 15

The poor sinners praying sincerely in the back of the Temple
will find God's favor more easily than the clergy in the front
who are just going through the motions.
Luke 18:14

Conventional wisdom turns to clerical personnel as repre-
senting true religion. Jesus looks with different eyes, God's
eyes, seeing what's behind the scene. He often finds God-
centeredness more with those who are in the back of the
Temple than with those who parade in fine robes in the front.

Daily Prayer

*Help me to pray today with my heart, not just
with my mouth.*

September 16

Will not justice be granted to those who cry to
God day and night?
Luke 18:7

There are so many things we wish for in the course of the day,
so many consumer products that the media has convinced us
we can't live without. But do we really cry to God for the just
world God wants to call into being?

Daily Prayer

Help me to make Your priorities mine today.

September 17

When I come, will I find faith on earth?
Luke 18:8

This is not a question for some distant day of judgment.
Only faith offers the receptive soil for Christ consciousness.
One day we will have evolved to the point where the whole
world will be filled with that consciousness, that intense
awareness of God.

Daily Prayer

I pray that in me You may always find faith.

September 18

What is impossible for mortals is possible for God.
Luke 18:26

Napoleon once said that the word "impossible" should not be in the French language. He, of course, was proved wrong, for there was much that became impossible for the little corporal and his French-speaking followers. But it is true that the word "impossible" is not in God's language and that's the point of Jesus' message.

Daily Prayer

Let me never despair about the future to which You call me.

September 19

I will be handed over to the Gentiles, mocked, insulted,
spat upon, flogged, and killed; but I will rise again
on the third day.
Luke 18:33

Good Friday is real; so too is Easter Sunday. Darkness and
dawn, suffering and joy, death and resurrection—Jesus' life
exhibits the deep rhythms of all human experience. In one
way or another, we will all go through this pattern.

Daily Prayer

*Lead me today from suffering to joy and from
death to resurrection.*

September 20

What do you want me to do for you?
Luke 18:41

It's sobering to realize that we really do have a good chance of getting what we want in many instances. That's why it's important to know what we want. Jesus doesn't enter obtrusively into a human life; he pauses to ask how the person wants to be helped.

Daily Prayer

Help me to want the right things today, whatever is truly best for me and for others.

September 21

Receive your sight; your faith has healed you.
Luke 18:42

Trust in God can help us to see the world and our fellow human beings with new eyes. There are so many forms of personal and societal blindness from which we need to be healed.

Daily Prayer

I trust You today to open my eyes so that I may truly see.

September 22

Zacchaeus, hurry and come down; I want to stay in
your house today.
Luke 19:5

Jesus bids this tax collector in a tree to come down and be his
host. Inviting his fellow tax collectors to a dinner in Jesus'
honor, Zacchaeus later tells Jesus that he will give back to
the poor the money he has extorted from them beyond their
legitimate taxes.

Daily Prayer

*Help me to realize that I am the steward of Your goods, not
their owner.*

September 23

Today salvation has come to this house, because this tax collector is also a son of Abraham.
Luke 19:9

Jesus praises Zacchaeus because he has repented of the extortion which characterized most of the tax collectors of this period. He has also promised restitution and a changed life in the future. This is what salvation and healing are all about.

Daily Prayer

I pray that salvation may come to my house today.

September 24

This is what I have come for, to search out and save
what is lost.
Luke 19:10

Jesus derives a special joy from seeing those people open up to God who, from the viewpoint of their society, are seen to be farthest from God. Tax collectors, slaves, prostitutes, the sick and deformed—these are examples of the marginalized people that the "decent folks" judged to be most godless.

Daily Prayer

Today may I show a special sensitivity to those people society judges as worthless and undeserving.

September 25

If these people were silent, the stones would shout out.
Luke 19:40

Jesus is greeted by the crowds as he enters Jerusalem to celebrate Passover. Many in that crowd had personally experienced the liberating power of Jesus' teaching and of his healing ministry. And yet, the clerical leaders are jealous that God is being met in a lay person of no official standing. It is to them that Jesus addresses these words, affirming that God deserves our praise and thanks for being the source of all life and beauty.

Daily Prayer

Let me not fail to praise and thank the Ground of Being for all the wonders of this day.

September 26

If you, Jerusalem, could only understand today all the ways
that can bring you peace.
Luke 19:42

Jerusalem, a city occupied by the Romans, was caught up in
supporting Caesar's reign rather than God's. Many of its citizens failed to discern that shalom/peace (a word that's in the
very name Jerusalem) can only be achieved through
God's justice.

Daily Prayer

Help me to discern the ways that lead to true peace today,
both in my life and in that of our restless world.

September 27

It is written: "My house shall be a house of prayer; but you
have made it a den of robbers."
Luke 19:46

Angered by the commercialization of religion in the House of
his Heavenly Parent, Jesus turns over the tables of the money
changers and releases the doves that are the offerings of the
poor. Profiteering is never more despicable than when it's done
in the name of religion.

Daily Prayer

*Help me to keep any place that bears Your name a place of
prayer, not of profit.*

September 28

In the resurrection from the dead, marriage no longer
has any relevance.
Luke 20:35

We can barely grasp the meaning of the lives we live now.
How can we possibly understand the life God holds out to us
in the future? We need to trust God in this matter and not let
our imaginations run too far in trying to describe the mystery.

Daily Prayer

Help me to trust You today and at the hour of my death.

September 29

The Torah implies resurrection in addressing God as the God of Abraham, of Isaac, and of Jacob; for God is the God of the living, not of the dead.

Luke 20:37-38

This is an important affirmation that those who have passed on before us continue to be alive in God. This is not something we can fully grasp but it is the basis for what is taught as "the communion of saints."

Daily Prayer

Help me to realize that those who have gone before me continue to be with me to help me along my way.

September 30

Watch out for those who like to parade around in clerical garb, loving to be called by their titles, and having the places of honor.
Luke 20:46

One of Jesus' most consistent themes is the abuse of clerical position and power. How often we see evidences of this today in our newspaper headlines and on our TV news. Official religion often puts institutions ahead of people; this leads inevitably to the abuse of those "little ones" who were so dear to Jesus' heart.

Daily Prayer

Help those who represent our religious institutions to be faithful to their call.

October 1

God's reign is like treasure hidden in a field. Anyone finding
it is eager to sell everything else to buy that field.
Matthew 13:44

Whatever would entice a merchant to buy something in
exchange for his whole inventory would have to be really spec-
tacular. Our participation in the divine life cannot stand on a
par with other values and goals; it must tower over all of them
in its centrality and importance.

Daily Prayer

*Help me to let go of anything today that would lessen my
participation in Your reign and the accomplishment
of Your will.*

October 2

This poor widow has given more to charity than
anyone else today.
Luke 21:3

Teaching in the Temple courtyard, Jesus notices a widow with
little money to spare placing a small coin into the poor box.
He stops in amazement at the generosity of her gift. The coin
was indeed small but her heart was great and
generous that day.

Daily Prayer

*Whether I have much or little to give to others, let me give
all that I can with a generous heart.*

October 3

Days of destruction are coming when not one of these Temple
stones will be left on another.
Luke 21:6

Jeremiah had foreseen the destruction of the First Temple
almost six hundred years earlier. Now Jesus foresees the
destruction of the Second Temple which does indeed take
place some forty years after his death. In both cases, the
destruction comes from the attempt to find peace other than
under God's reign.

Daily Prayer

*Don't let me build my hopes on anything that doesn't have
You as its foundation.*

October 4

Many will come using my name to say that the end of the world is coming. Don't be led astray.
Luke 21:8

The turn of a millennium tempts many to seek a calendar of the end events. This is all distraction and delusion. God calls us to be attentive to the present moment and the inbreak of God's reign in the here and now.

Daily Prayer

Don't let me be led astray by calculations of future events; let me rather direct all my attention to doing Your will in this present moment.

October 5

I promise you that today you'll be with me in Paradise.
Luke 23:43

The dying request of the repentant thief is granted by Jesus, demonstrating that no one is ever more than one breath away from God's forgiving love. Even in his final moments on the cross, Jesus reaches out to others with compassion and mercy.

Daily Prayer

In You I enjoy eternal life, both in this world and beyond.

October 6

This generation will not pass away until all these
things have taken place.
Luke 21:32

A biblical generation is counted as forty years and the destruction of the Second Temple took place forty years after Jesus'
prophecy. A public policy not founded on the pursuit of justice will inevitably lead to disaster. Hitler's vaunted Thousand
Year Reich crumbled in little more than a decade.

Daily Prayer

*Help me to realize that no viable future for myself or
society can be achieved in any way other than by the
pursuit of justice.*

October 7

Be attentive, praying that you have the strength to escape all
these things and to remain in my presence.
Luke 21:36

Innocent individuals sometimes suffer disaster in the collapse
of unjust societies. We can't privatize our lives by denying our
involvement with the larger communities in which we participate: religious organizations, families, neighborhoods, cities,
countries, and the planetary community itself.

Daily Prayer

*Let me work to help the societies in which I live; but if they
collapse, let me nonetheless remain with You.*

October 8

Go and prepare the Passover meal for us that we may eat it.
Luke 22:8

Knowing that the end of his earthly career is near, Jesus wants
to share this special holiday meal with the community of
those closest to him. It is a festival of hope, celebrating God's
liberating love in leading people in every generation from
slavery to freedom.

Daily Prayer

*Let me celebrate in my life today Your will to bring us all
from slavery to freedom.*

October 9

I have eagerly desired to eat this Passover with you before I suffer, since I won't eat it again until it finds its fulfillment in God's reign.
Luke 22:15-16

The final liberation signified by the Passover meal will only be celebrated when human history has ended and humankind enters into the fullness of God's reign. It is important to Jesus, especially because of the suffering ahead of him, to share the joy of this Jewish holiday with his friends.

Daily Prayer

Help me to find joy in the moments of this day, even when suffering and hardship follow in their wake.

October 10

Take this cup and share it, for I won't drink wine again until
God's reign comes.
Luke 22:17-18

The full cup of wine in the Jewish tradition is a sign of the
fullness of God's messianic reign. As Jesus shares this cup of
blessing with his closest community of friends, he is reminded
of the final fullness that can be found only at the end of
human history.

Daily Prayer

*Let me taste in every joy of this day an anticipation of the
fullness of joy that awaits us all in the fullness of time.*

October 11

Where your treasure is, there your heart will be as well.
Gospel Q 54

What is our highest priority—our job, money, sex, food, fame,
friends, or something else? Our answer reveals our true god,
for that's our treasure, our heart's center and our highest goal.

Daily Prayer

With all my Muslim brothers and sisters,
let me remind myself at least five times today that
there is no God but God.

October 12

It is a blessing to be pure in heart; you will see God.
Gospel Q 12

The Danish philosopher Kierkegaard claimed that purity of heart means to will one thing. But the only thing big enough and deep enough to encompass our every moment is the divine reality, the mystery we call God's will.

Daily Prayer

As the tasks and challenges of this day change, let me remain steadfastly focused purely on Your will.

October 13

What God has put together let no one separate.
Mark 10:9

A marriage that is truly rooted in the divine reality will not easily fall apart. And yet so many unions today are based on little more than convenience or codependence. Putting the divine first in a relationship is always a challenge.

Daily Prayer

Help me to add You to the formula for all my relationships this day.

October 14

You certainly consider the host of a dinner as more important than the one who serves at the table; and yet, I am among you as one who serves.
Luke 22:27

Jesus is sometimes called "the man for others." It is staggering to realize how totally he lives his life as one who serves. What a contrast to our society where people step on others in climbing the corporate ladder to get to the top.

Daily Prayer

Help me to live this day as one who serves.

October 15

Pray that you may not come into the time of trial.
Luke 22:40

Trials and tests are part of human life; they can't be totally avoided. We can pray that we not falter or fail in these times of testing but that we persevere in walking a God-centered path of justice, peace, and compassion.

Daily Prayer

Don't let me be tested beyond my strength and don't let me be defeated in any trials that await me.

October 16

Heavenly Parent, if you are willing, remove this cup from me;
yet, not my will but yours be done.
Luke 22:42

Jesus is no masochist. He neither delights in suffering nor
desires it. But his obedience to God's will and God's way has
put him on a collision course with the might of Rome. Arrest
and execution await him.

Daily Prayer

*If my path today must include suffering, then let me accept
it in Your name.*

October 17

Why are you sleeping? Get up and pray that you may not
come into the time of trial.
Luke 22:46

Facing times of trial is difficult enough but being abandoned
by close friends at those times increases the pain a hundred-
fold. Jesus realizes, of course, that this time of trial affects the
lives of his followers too and he asks them to be prepared for
what lies ahead of them as well.

Daily Prayer

*I pray that with Your help I will be ready for any trials
I must face today.*

October 18

What are you discussing with each other while
you walk along?
Luke 24:17

Two disciples are walking along after Jesus' death. They feel
despair and abandonment, unable to understand God's ways in
all that has transpired. The risen Jesus, unrecognized by them,
approaches and encourages them to share their story.

Daily Prayer

*Help me to recognize You hidden in the many encounters of
this day.*

October 19

Was it not necessary that the Messiah should suffer these
things and then enter into his glory?
Luke 24:26

Speaking to these two discouraged disciples, Jesus explains to
them that even the Messiah had to suffer in obeying God and
doing God's work in the world. Sometimes suffering is the
only door to growth.

Daily Prayer

*Help me to be courageous in those times when it is only by
suffering that I can obey You and do Your will.*

October 20

Since you don't know the real nature of the letter "a," how do
you expect to teach the letter "b"?
Infancy Gospel of Thomas 6:19

Our initial point of entry is of crucial importance. If we have
no connection to the divine reality in the beginning of our
journey, how can we expect to show others the way? Or even
to take a second step ourselves?

Daily Prayer

*Let my first step today be the right one, so that all the others
may follow.*

October 21

Why are you frightened and why do doubts arise
in your hearts?
Luke 24:38

Even in the full flush of encountering Jesus victorious over death, there are those who fear and even doubt. Ambivalence runs like a stain through the cloth of human experience. Lack of faith dilutes our faith on almost every occasion.

Daily Prayer

I believe; please help my unbelief.

October 22

Look at my hands and my feet; see that it is I myself.
Luke 24:39

Jesus is risen but the body they see still bears the marks
of crucifixion. The Easter experience can never totally be
divorced from Good Friday. Death and resurrection form a
dynamic reality together.

Daily Prayer

*Let me not expect a crown without a cross, a God-filled life
without challenge and suffering.*

October 23

Let's go to some deserted place, just us, and rest awhile.
Mark 6:31

Incessant activity and busy-ness do not cultivate the soil in
which spiritual growth occurs. We need to make time for
solitude and silence, even a few moments in which we can sit
still, letting God be God.

Daily Prayer

May I find some quiet time today simply to be with God.

October 24

Heavenly Parent, the hour has come; glorify Your Son so that
the Son may glorify You.
John 17:1

In the crucible of suffering, Jesus discerns the glory of God
that is simultaneously present. There is no time when praising
God has more meaning than when our whole human reality
wants no part of singing God's praise.

Daily Prayer

*Help me to praise You in good times and in bad,
in sickness and in health.*

October 25

Whoever is not against us is for us.
Mark 9:40

We sometimes construe those walking another spiritual path than ours as enemies; they may instead be allies. Our instinct to clone our own spiritual experience finds its roots in our ego much more than in our God.

Daily Prayer

Open my eyes today to recognize all those who are doing Your will in the world, even when they look different from me or disagree with my ideas.

October 26

This is my commandment, that you love one another as
I have loved you.
John 15:12

The cornerstone of Christian ethics, this commandment leads
to the imitatio Christi (imitation of Christ) that is so central
to Christian spirituality. A Christian is one who tries in every
moment to live as Jesus lived and to love as Jesus loved.

Daily Prayer

*Help me to love my fellow human beings with a love that is
in some small way like Yours.*

October 27

Those who want to save their life will lose it but those who
lose their life will save it.
Mark 8:35

Like the egg from which the young chick emerges, the ego has
to break open if the self is to be revealed. The ego is the dis-
connected "I"; the self, on the other hand, is an "I" relating to
and including everything else in the universe. We need to let
go of the ego to find our identity in the deeper self.

Daily Prayer

*Help me to lose a little bit of my ego today and to find more
of my deeper self.*

October 28

Go out and bear fruit, fruit that lasts.
John 15:16b

So much of what we do is as transient as the morning news-paper. But whatever is done in true love is as eternal as the God whose very nature is love. The fruit of true love is indeed eternal fruit.

Daily Prayer

Help me to bear fruit today, fruit that lasts.

October 29

A little while and you will no longer see me and again a little
while and you will see me.
John 16:16

Jesus assures his frightened followers that they will experience
him once again after his death. And when that presence too
is removed, then the Holy Spirit will be given them as a gift
never to be taken away.

Daily Prayer

Keep me close to You today; bind me to You with Your spirit.

October 30

As You have sent me into the world, so I have sent them
into the world.
John 17:18

We have not been thrown into an absurd world but sent into
a disobedient world, a world that is often deep in denial and
distraction. We are in that world but not of it. And we are
never there alone.

Daily Prayer

Thank You for sending me into Your world today.

October 31

Eat your bread, my brother James, for I have been raised from among those who sleep.
Gospel of the Hebrews 9:4

St. Paul assures us too that the risen Jesus appeared to his brother, James. Here we find a saying of Jesus with which he greets his brother, the man who is to be the leader of the Jerusalem church for some thirty years until his martyrdom.

Daily Prayer

Let me too hear the words spoken in my own heart assuring me that God lives and the risen Jesus lives in God forever.

November 1

Come and see.
John 1:39

Jesus invites two of John the Baptist's disciples to come with him and see where he's staying. Andrew is one of the two and the other, though unnamed, may be the beloved disciple whose testimony is embedded in this gospel. The text does not tell us what transpired, only that they spent the day with Jesus.

Daily Prayer

Help me to spend this day with You, learning Your ways and experiencing Your love.

November 2

The wind blows where it chooses and you hear
the sound of it but you don't really know where it
comes from or where it goes.
John 3:8

In both Hebrew and Greek, the same word means both
"wind" and "spirit." God's spirit in the world, like the wind
that is its symbol, cannot be pinned down, contained, or
curbed. An important lesson for all of us when we want to
control the divine reality or make it behave according to the
needs of our ego.

Daily Prayer

*Help me to be truly open to Your spirit today, daring to go
wherever that spirit leads me.*

November 3

Give me a drink.
John 4:7

This woman at the well whom Jesus asks for a drink is triply marginalized. She is a Samaritan, a group most Jews avoided. She is a woman, whom respectable men would not address. Finally, she comes to the well at noon, a time when only disreputable women would be seen there. But Jesus once again shows himself to be a barrier breaker as he asks a favor of this woman, for he sees her too as God's daughter.

Daily Prayer

Help me to be a barrier breaker today as I meet the diverse people who are all counted among Your children.

November 4

My food is to do the will of the One who sent me and
to complete God's work.
John 4:34

Physical food and physical hunger were often images for Jesus
of a deeper food and a greater hunger. It is good to bless God
as we satisfy our physical hunger but it is even better to thank
God for nurturing the hunger of our souls.

Daily Prayer

*Give me the bread I need today, both bread for my body and
bread for my spiritual journey.*

November 5

But if you do not believe what Moses said, how will you
believe what I say?
John 5:47

What Jesus teaches is deeply embedded in the Hebrew scrip-
tures: the Torah from Moses, the prophetic writings, plus the
wisdom literature and the psalms. Although Jesus brings his
Jewish tradition together in a unique way, there is nothing in
what he says that repudiates it or suggests its replacement.

Daily Prayer

*Help me to be open to all Your words today and to see that
they form a message consistent with Your goodness and love*

November 6

Gather up the fragments left over so that
nothing may be lost.
John 6:13

The gospels love to repeat these stories of the multitudes
being fed. Perhaps these were situations where people learned
the true meaning of community: how to share, how to help
each other, how to make sure that nothing is wasted or lost.

Daily Prayer

*Help me to build true community today by my service to
others and my interaction with them at every level.*

November 7

It is me; don't be afraid.
John 6:20

Like his Heavenly Parent, Jesus wants full and abundant life for each person he encounters. Even when his presence and words cause discomfort and pain, they function like a surgeon's instrument in promoting health and wellbeing. There is nothing to fear from those who truly act on God's behalf.

Daily Prayer

Don't let me be afraid of Your action in my life today, even when You take me to places in myself where I am trying to hide from You.

November 8

Do not judge by appearances, but judge
with right judgment.
John 7:24

It is exceedingly difficult in our society to see beyond
appearances. What people wear, what they drive, how they
look—these are the measures of worth and prestige in our
media-created culture. It's a real challenge to see beyond an
unattractive face, shabby clothes, an accent,
a skin color, or a sexual orientation.

Daily Prayer

Let me move beyond appearances in meeting people today.

November 9

Let anyone among you without sin be the first to throw a
stone at her.
John 8:7

Like Jesus' teaching about seeing the speck in another's eye
while neglecting the beam in one's own, his words challenge
those who would stone the woman taken in adultery. Why is
it so much easier for us to see the sins of others than our own?

Daily Prayer

Don't let me get caught up in judging people today.

November 10

I judge no one.
John 8:15

These words make it clear that Jesus' role is not to judge but to heal and make whole. How often those of us who claim the name "Christian" are recognized more by our harsh judgments of others than by our compassion.

Daily Prayer

When the temptation to judge another arises in me today, let me replace it with thoughts of compassion.

November 11

The truth will make you free.
John 8:31

Truth here is not what lives above our eyebrows, i.e.,
"two plus two is four" truth. It is the experienced and
transformative truth that changes lives. To appropriate fully
the truth that Jesus teaches leads us to a profound
realization of freedom.

Daily Prayer

*Let me participate in Your freedom today, and not live
in the restricted quarters of this world's judgments and
categories.*

November 12

Heavenly Parent, I thank You for having heard me now, just
as You have always heard me.
John 11:42

Jesus' words here reflect the deepest theology of prayer. Prayer
is not a matter of trying to persuade or bribe God to hear us.
God already is more on our side than we are. No prayer goes
unanswered; and yet, the answer relates to our deepest self,
not to the expectations of our superficial ego.

Daily Prayer

*Let me open my heart to You today with the confidence that
no prayer of mine will ever be unanswered.*

November 13

Whoever believes in me, believes not in me but the one
who sent me.
John 12:44

Many of Jesus' teachings deflect attention from himself to
the One who sends him. The ultimate faith of a Christian lies
not in Jesus but in the God with whom Jesus connects us.
Religion persistently confuses the finger pointing to the moon
with the moon, and this often has tragic consequences when
we deal with people of other faiths.

Daily Prayer

*Let me be attentive today to the many signs of Your reality
and Your truth.*

November 14

You do not know what I am doing but later
you will understand.
John 13:7

Jesus' actions were so often misinterpreted by his disciples
because they were caught up in their own ego needs. Will
Jesus do magical tricks? Will he drive out the Romans who
occupy the land? Will he give special perks to his disciples?

Daily Prayer

*Help me to trust the fact that the results of trying to do Your
will today may only be understood by me later.*

November 15

So if I have washed your feet, you ought to wash
one another's feet.
John 13:14

At the last meal he shares with his friends, Jesus performs the role of a servant by washing their feet. Even at the very end, he lives as the man for others; he models the service that is to characterize the lives of his disciples. His teachings challenge us to transform the drive to dominate into the impulse to serve.

Daily Prayer

*Help me truly to serve others today, not trying to
control them.*

November 16

If you know these things, you are blessed if you do them.
John 13:17

The blessing does not consist simply in having the knowledge in our minds; the blessing comes when the teachings are implemented in our lives. It is not enough to hear God's words; we must do them. The tree is known by its fruit.

Daily Prayer

Help me to do at least some of what I know today.

November 17

By this love everyone will know you are my disciples, if you
have love for one another.
John 13:35

Love should be the criterion of any community that bears
Jesus' name. And yet, how many religious wars, witch hunts,
crusades, and pogroms have been carried out in his name or
even under the banner of his cross?

Daily Prayer

*Let love be at the forefront of all my dealings with
others today.*

November 18

I tell you that the one who believes in me will do the works
that I do and will do greater works than these.
John 14:12

How can we do greater works than Jesus did? Only by realizing that of ourselves we can do nothing, although with God
we can indeed do all things. The great sixteenth-century mystic, Teresa of Avila, used to say that she was nothing by herself
but everything with God.

Daily Prayer

*Do great things in me today, even when You must do them
despite me.*

November 19

As God has loved me, so I have loved you;
abide in my love.
John 15:9

What an extraordinary claim. Few can say with Jesus that they love others as fully as God loves them. And this love is to be our home, the place where we abide, the consciousness that remains with us through all of life's changes and challenges.

Daily Prayer

Let nothing distract me from abiding in Your love today.

November 20

Ask and you will receive.
John 16:24

How often Jesus speaks of the absolute confidence that we should have in prayer. No conditions are attached to this promise. We will always receive all that we need to be the self God is calling into being in each moment. Only our egos will sometimes be disappointed with the way our prayers are answered.

Daily Prayer

Give me all that I need today to be all that You want me to be.

November 21

Whom are you looking for?
John 18:5

Each age launches a new quest for the historical Jesus. And yet, who is it that we are seeking? A mere historical personage or someone who continues to have the power to transform lives by every word that he taught and every deed he accomplished?

Daily Prayer

Let me look for Your transforming power in every moment of my life today.

November 22

Put your sword back into its sheath.
John 18:11

Jesus' arrest is not to be stopped by the sword. Violence rarely achieves what it seeks. What do we teach when we hit a child for hitting its sibling or kill a criminal for killing a fellow human being? We have to break through the cycle of violence the way Jesus did.

Daily Prayer

Let me not rush for the violent resolution to the problems I encounter today but let me try to follow Your path to conflict resolution and peace.

November 23

I have said nothing in secret.
John 18:20

A Zen Buddhist teacher claims that there are no secret sayings, only secret ears. We hear as much truth as we allow ourselves to hear. There is no lack of spiritual teaching, only a lack of hearing and doing.

Daily Prayer

Open my mind today fully to hear all that You are teaching me.

November 24

Woman, here is your son.
John 19:26

On the cross, Jesus entrusts his mother to his beloved disciple. A woman needed the protection of a man's home in the patriarchal culture in which Jesus lived. With Joseph dead, Mary needed someone to provide for her. So even in the agony of death, Jesus takes care of others.

Daily Prayer

Help me look out for the needs of others today, even when I'm feeling discomfort or pain.

November 25

I am thirsty.
John 19:28

Jesus is human to the end, even in his thirst on the cross. He is not a phantom, not a god walking on earth, following a script, and pretending to be human. He is a true human being in whom the divine reality is fully manifest.

Daily Prayer

Let me cherish all my human feelings this day, knowing that they are avenues to You and Your will for me.

November 26

It is finished.
John 19:30

How fortunate any of us would be to die knowing that our work is finished, that our life has reached completeness. It is not dying that people fear but not having lived. Today is the opportunity at hand for living in such a way that we can have Jesus' consciousness of completion when we die.

Daily Prayer

Help me to live my life fully today, with nothing left over or undone.

November 27

Woman, why are you weeping?
John 20:13

Jesus' death is not a tragedy. It opens up a new springtime for God's spirit in the world. It provides for a more extensive experience of Jesus' life and teachings to countless people in every subsequent age of human history.

Daily Prayer

Let me live this day as an Easter person, trusting the power of life over death.

November 28

Peace be with you.
John 20:26

Shalom—the Hebrew word that means "wholeness,"
"completion," "peace," "hello," and "goodbye." Everything
has come full in Jesus' life and death, in his teachings and in
his deeds of compassion. His disciples receive now the gift of
completeness, of peace.

Daily Prayer

*May I know peace today and may I be an instrument of
peace for others.*

November 29

If you forgive the sins of any, they are forgiven.
John 20:23

Just as God offers future to us, despite our mistakes, so do we have the power to offer future to others. The disciples of Jesus are called to do all that Jesus did, and more. Jesus outlined a blueprint of something that will be under construction until the last day of human history.

Daily Prayer

Let me turn to others today with the same spirit of forgiveness that You show to me.

November 30

Blessed are those who have not seen and yet still believe.
John 20:29

We sometimes envy those who lived when Jesus walked the earth, but the great Danish philosopher and religious thinker, Soren Kierkegaard, claims that each of us has the opportunity to be a contemporary of Jesus. Whoever listens to his teachings is present to him more than those who merely shared his physical world.

Daily Prayer

Let me be blessed for trusting You in all the circumstances of my day.

December 1

Recognize what is in front of your face, and what is concealed
will be revealed to you. For there is nothing hidden that will
not be disclosed.
Gospel of Thomas 5

The way to what is not in front of us always takes us through
what is in front of us. There is no way to the next moment
except through the here and now. There is no shortcut to what
is hidden; we must walk the extraordinary
path of the ordinary.

Daily Prayer

Help me today truly to know what is in front of my face.

December 2

Humankind is like a wise fisherman who casts his net into the sea. He drew it out of the sea full of small fish. The wise fisherman found among them a large, good fish. He threw all the small fish back into the sea and chose the large fish without hesitation. Whoever has ears to hear, let him hear.
Gospel of Thomas 8

Jesus teaches so frequently from the ordinary experiences of the people with whom he lived and worked. Someone seeking a good dinner for his family is certainly willing to throw back any little fish once he has found the big fish that will serve as the main course at his dinner table.

Daily Prayer

Help me to know the difference between the little fish that I haul in today and the truly big fish that is found in my net.

December 3

I have cast fire on the world and, look, I am guarding it
until it blazes.
Gospel of Thomas 10

Jesus employs a shocking image here. Certainly a spreading
fire threatens life and safety. So too does the wisdom that Jesus
teaches. Subversive wisdom is not at all like the caress of a
summer breeze but like a blast of desert heat.

Daily Prayer

*Let Your fire burn in me today, consuming all that stands
in the way of Your will.*

December 4

No prophet is acceptable in his own village; a physician does
not heal those who know him.
Gospel of Thomas 31

Psychiatrists don't treat their family members, anymore than
surgeons operate on their loved ones. The "scholar in resi-
dence" never comes from the neighborhood. And yet it sometimes makes sense to listen to the one who is close at hand.

Daily Prayer

*Help me to hear Your word, even when it comes from
someone close to me.*

December 5

A city built on a high mountain and well-fortified cannot fall,
nor can it remain hidden.
Gospel of Thomas 32

What Jesus taught is for the world's healing. These truths
should not be hidden in arcane books but shouted from the
housetops. These teachings make strong dwelling places for
the human spirit.

Daily Prayer

***Let Your truth in me be a strong and visible city on
a hill today.***

December 6

Do not be anxious, from morning to evening and from evening to morning, about what you will wear.
Gospel of Thomas 36

One doesn't have to walk far to meet many well-dressed crooks and con artists. What an enlightened society we would be if we paid half as much attention to what is in our hearts as we do to what is in our closets.

Daily Prayer

Help me to see my soul in the mirror today more frequently than my body.

December 7

A vine was planted without the father, but because it did not
become strong it will be uprooted and will rot.
Gospel of Thomas 40

Much like the teaching in John's gospel about the organic
unity of vine and branches, here we find a metaphor built on
the union of vine and soil. God is indeed, in Paul Tillich's tell-
ing phrase, "the Ground of Being."

Daily Prayer

Let all that I do today be rooted and planted in You.

December 8

He who has come to understand the world has found a corpse;
and the world is not worthy of him who has found a corpse.
Gospel of Thomas 56

"Finding a corpse" was a Jewish expression of praise. The
world in this teaching is not the created world of birds and
flowers but the socialized world that forms a grid over much
of our experience. This world of conventional wisdom is often
a lifeless form and an empty shell. We're lucky if we come to
understand it for what it is.

Daily Prayer

*Let me not be caught up today in the empty world of societal
norms and expectations.*

December 9

Show me the stone that the builders rejected.
That is the cornerstone.
Gospel of Thomas 66

What a striking image. The very stone that is discarded by the builders is the true foundation stone of what God wants to build. The problem comes when we judge reality from the human instead of from the divine perspective.

Daily Prayer

Let me not throw away what society discards before knowing whether or not it is part of what You are building.

December 10

The harvest is great but the laborers are few, so pray to the
Lord to send laborers to the harvest.
Gospel of Thomas 73

People are standing in line to exploit and take advantage of
their fellow human beings but there aren't many who truly
want to serve them. And yet that is precisely what Jesus
challenges his followers to do. That is the true harvest
Jesus wants to see.

Daily Prayer

Let me be among those who truly want to serve others.

December 11

Lord, there are many standing around the drinking trough,
but there is nothing in the well.
Gospel of Thomas 74

Not all those talking so eagerly into their car phones are
imparting wisdom. Not all those downloading information at
their computers are receiving wisdom. Our societal drinking
troughs are often bone dry. We still need living water.

Daily Prayer

*Help me to find the water today that can satisfy
my thirst forever.*

December 12

Blessed are those who have heard the word of the father and
have truly kept it.
Gospel of Thomas 79

Our society thinks that it's the height of luck to win the
lottery or some million dollar sweepstakes. But the greater
blessing is to hear the word of God and keep it. And keeping
t doesn't mean hiding it but translating it into all our words
and deeds.

Daily Prayer

*Help me to hear Your word today above the noise and din of
society's empty chatter; and help me to do all that I hear.*

December 13

Let him who has become rich become king, and let him who
has power renounce it.
Gospel of Thomas 81

The operative words are coded to a counter-cultural message.
The truly wealthy, the truly powerful are those who are rich
in knowing God and powerful in serving others. The kind of
wealth and power that society cultivates and clings to has no
place in the world that God calls into being.

Daily Prayer

*Help me to be rich and powerful today by my true
service to others.*

December 14

The foxes have their dens and the birds have their nests, but
the son of man has nowhere to lay his head and rest.
Gospel of Thomas 86

Life is a bridge; we must pass over it but not build our
houses on it. The carrier of subversive wisdom is always
marginalized to some extent—like prophets and poets, like
mystics and monks. A follower of Jesus' teaching is always a
work in progress.

Daily Prayer

*Help me to resist the seduction of being settled and rigid,
fixed to one idea and powerless to move.*

December 15

Come to me, for my yoke is easy and my lordship is gentle
and you will find repose for yourselves.
Gospel of Thomas 90

This is a dramatic image of the paradox of Jesus' teaching. It
is at once a way of the cross and a comfortable yoke. The pain
stays mainly with our egos; the comfort comes in knowing the
deeper part of ourselves that is yoked to the divine.

Daily Prayer

*Thank you for sharing Your yoke with me today and
making my way easier.*

December 16

Whoever searches will find. It will be opened to him.
Gospel of Thomas 94

This teaching brings great encouragement. No sincere prayer
will be unanswered. Even if the answer represents a "no" to
our ego agenda, it will always be a "yes" to the needs of our
deepest self.

Daily Prayer

*Let my searching heart open today to find in You what I
most deeply seek.*

December 17

If you have money, do not lend it at interest, but give to those
from whom you will not receive it back.
Gospel of Thomas 95

Our conventional wisdom is shaken. A loan officer wouldn't
last long without demanding collateral. But God's ways are
not society's ways and God's challenge to us often entails
reversing the order of our societal conditioning.

Daily Prayer

*Help me to trust Your wisdom over that of the pundits of
our secular society.*

December 18

Let him who has found the world and become rich
deny the world.
Gospel of Thomas 110

The crux of this teaching revolves around the word "world."
This is not the created world which God in Genesis pro-
nounces good but the socialized world constructed by our all-
too-human perspectives and prejudices. When people have the
real wealth of the spirit, they are in a position to renounce the
empty socialized world.

Daily Prayer

*Help me to let go of my attachment to the fads and fashions
of my society and find the true wealth of Your words and
Your wisdom.*

December 19

Yours is life.
Secret Book of James 3:6

This is the final proof: fuller and more abundant life.
So many teachings seem to leave people anxious, afraid of
other opinions, constricted in their thinking. The teachings o
Jesus expand us, enlighten us, empower us.

Daily Prayer

*Give me life today, the true and abundant life that only
You can give.*

December 20

Therefore become full and leave no place
within you empty.
Secret Book of James 3:11

There is a good emptiness which is receptivity and a bad
emptiness which is mere lack, just as there is a good fullness
which is God's wisdom and a bad fullness which is the chatter
of our socialized world.

Daily Prayer

*Give me the fullness of life in You and take from me the
emptiness of mere ego.*

December 21

Therefore become full of the spirit but lacking in reason.
Secret Book of James 3:18

Spirituality affirms a two-fold transition. First we move from
the irrational to the rational; but then we must move from the
rational to the trans-rational. At this final level, mere reason is
transcended by the fuller life of the spirit.

Daily Prayer

*Help me to be rational enough to know when to let go of
what is only rational.*

December 22

Become better than I.
Secret Book of James 5:6

Words like this coming from Jesus can have no meaning for Christians who have been taught that a life of faith is a diminished life, a frightened and guilt-ridden life, a life cowering in corners for fear of making mistakes. But for Christians who have ears to hear, this is the best teaching of all.

Daily Prayer

Let me aspire to be better than Moses, better than Jesus, better than the Buddha. Let me aspire to be nothing less than You in me.

December 23

Become haters of hypocrisy and evil intent.
Secret Book of James 6:8

When our words and our deeds move in different directions,
we are a scandal to God and humankind alike. Better a small
step that is honest than a giant step that is a lie.

Daily Prayer

*Help me to want only what is good and to do only
what is honest.*

December 24

Become eager for instruction.
Secret Book of James 6:16

The challenge of teaching is not to have answers but to tease out the questions for which the answers exist. To engage in real learning we must have an appetite for instruction.

Daily Prayer

Give me an appetite for what I can learn from Your spirit, an eagerness for what I can eat and drink at wisdom's table.

December 25

Never be glad unless you look at your brother or
sister with love.
Gospel of the Hebrews 7

Christmas is love's birthday. Any discipleship that bears the
name of the one whose birthday is commemorated this day
must be a discipleship of love; otherwise,
it is a pretense and a lie.

Daily Prayer

In whatever else I may fail, let me love today.

December 26

Don't be arrogant about the light that enlightens.
Secret Book of James 8:10

A Buddhist teacher speaks of "spiritual materialism," our clinging to some notion of "spiritual progress" and "enlightenment." Preening ourselves on spiritual gifts betrays their absence. The deepest spiritual life is ordinary.

Daily Prayer

Don't let me get caught clinging to the good You choose to accomplish through me.

December 27

Many will come using my name claiming: "I'm the one."
Mark 13:6

Countless people claim to speak for God, to be God's official voice in the world. How do we separate the prophets from the charlatans? God's language is love and only those who speak in love speak for God.

Daily Prayer

Let all my words today be spoken in love.

December 28

Whatever is from woman, dies; whatever is from the truth
does not die.
Dialogue of the Savior 23:2

When Mohammed died, one of his friends told the people
assembled nearby: "For those of you who worship Mohammed,
know that Mohammed is dead; for those of you who worship
God, know that God is alive."

Daily Prayer

Let me be captive to Your truth for that alone does not die.

December 29

Stand in the place you can reach.
Dialogue of the Savior 30

The perfect can be the enemy of the good. People dream about how holy they could be in a monastery or nursing lepers in Calcutta, but fail to see the real step that is there for them to take in the here and now.

Daily Prayer

Let me stand in the place I can reach; let me walk on the path that is in front of me.

December 30

Heavenly Parent, into your hands I entrust my spirit.
Luke 23:46

Trust in the divine reality is the beginning and the end of
every spiritual path. Faith is the way we trust our life forward,
even to its last moment.

Daily Prayer

entrust this day to You and I put my spirit in Your hands.

December 31

I am the Alpha and the Omega, the first and the last, the
beginning and the end.
Revelation 22:13

The Cosmic Christ, God's Word and God's Deed in the world,
announces that all beginnings and all endings come from
God, exist in God, and tend towards God.

Daily Prayer

*May this year end in God's mercy and may the new year
begin in God's power.*

Further Reading

—For a good introduction to the historical Jesus and the distinction between conventional and subversive wisdom: Marcus Borg's Meeting Jesus Again for the First Time (San Francisco, CA: Harper, 1995).

—For another provocative introduction to the historical Jesus: John Dominic Crossan's Jesus: A Revolutionary Biography (San Francisco, CA: Harper, 1994).

—For information on the gospels that are not in the Christian Testament: The Complete Gospels, ed. Robert J. Miller (Sonoma, CA: Polebridge Press, 1992).

—For an approach to the spirituality underlying the message of Jesus: Ron Miller's "Space for the Spirit" in Finding a Way, ed. J. Zirker (Boston, MA: Tuttle, 1996).

—The quotations from The Gospel of Thomas are from The Apocryphal New Testament, ed. J. K. Elliott (Oxford: Oxford University Press, 1993).

—The quotations from The Q Gospel are numbered according to The Lost Gospel Q: The Original Sayings of Jesus, ed. Marcus Borg (Berkeley, CA: Seastone/Ulysses Press, 1996).

Made in the USA
Lexington, KY
25 September 2011